Franklin D. Roosevelt

Allan M. Winkler

Miami University

Franklin D. Roosevelt
and the Making of Modern America

THE LIBRARY OF AMERICAN BIOGRAPHY

Edited by Mark C. Carnes

New York   Boston   San Francisco
London   Toronto   Sydney   Tokyo   Singapore   Madrid
Mexico City   Munich   Paris   Cape Town   Hong Kong   Montreal

Executive Editor: Michael Boezi
Executive Marketing Manager: Sue Westmoreland
Production Coordinator: Virginia Riker
Cover Design Manager: John Callahan
Cover Image: Courtesy of the National Organization of Disability,
    Washington D.C.
Visual Researcher: Rona Tuccillo
Senior Manufacturing Buyer: Alfred C. Dorsey
Electronic Page Makeup: Alison Barth Burgoyne
Printer and Binder: RR Donnelley and Sons Company / Harrisonburg
Cover Printer: Phoenix Color

Photo Credits: p. ii, courtesy of Franklin Delano Roosevelt Library;
p. 82, courtesy of AP Worldwide Photos; p. 129, courtesy of Franklin
Delano Roosevelt Library; p. 177, courtesy of AP Worldwide photos.

Library of Congress Cataloging-in-Publication Data

Winkler, Allan M.,
    Franklin D. Roosevelt and the making of modern America / Allan
M. Winkler.
        p. cm. — (Library of American Biography)
    Includes bibliographical references and index.
        ISBN 0-321-09114-0
    1. Roosevelt, Franklin D. (Franklin Delano), 1882–1945. 2.
Presidents—United States—Biography. 3. United States—Politics
and government—1933–1945. 4. New Deal, 1933–1939. 5.
World War, 1939–1945—United States. 6. Governors—New
York (State)—Biography. I. Title. II. Series: Library of American
Biography (New York, N.Y.)

E807.W584 2005
973.917'092—dc22   2005005596

Copyright © 2006 by Pearson Education, Inc.

Visit our website at http://www.ablongman.com

ISBN 0-321-09114-0

    3 4 5 6 7 8 9 10—DOH—08 07 06

*For
Drew and Mary
and
Karl and Karen*

Contents

Editor's Preface

I am delighted to be the new general editor for the distinguished Library of American Biography series. Having served as editor of the American National Biography, I recognize the value of using biography to bring history to life, and I appreciate the opportunity and the challenge of my new role. To offer readers concise, interpretative biographies of individuals whose actions and ideas have significantly influenced the course of American history and national life remains the goal of the Library of American Biography series. Oscar Handlin, the original editor for the series, set a lofty standard with the many fine biographies that he commissioned. *Franklin D. Roosevelt and the Making of Modern America*, the first volume to be published under my aegis, will—I trust—confirm that the series will continue to meet that standard.

"Some are born great, some achieve greatness, and some have greatness thrust upon 'em," Shakespeare observed. Few presidents have generated more controversy than Franklin Delano Roosevelt. But nearly all observers concur that he was a titanic figure in twentieth century America. What's more, he acquired greatness in all three ways cited by Shakespeare.

Born into a family of tremendous wealth and power, FDR seemed destined for great things even as a child. His rise in New York politics was patterned after that of his famous cousin, President Theodore Roosevelt. When FDR became assistant secretary of the Navy, he sat at the same desk Theodore Roosevelt had occupied several decades earlier. "The delightful significance of it all is just beginning to dawn on me," FDR remarked.

Many young men, similarly possessed of wealth and great expectations, do not attain greatness. When, at 39, FDR was struck by polio, he achieved the requisite strength of character while overcoming the crippling effects of the disease.

Greatness, too, was thrust upon him when, as president, he confronted two of the nation's gravest challenges: the Great Depression and the Second World War.

To compress so complex and influential a life is a daunting challenge. In this concise book, historian Allan M. Winkler briskly recounts the subtle interplay of FDR's complex personality and the major political, economic and diplomatic events of his time. The marriage of the ebullient Franklin and the shy Eleanor has been the subject of many fat volumes, but Winkler addresses the matter with admirable brevity. After relating how Eleanor told her young husband of her disappointments with their marriage, Winkler concludes that Franklin "listened but found it hard to understand her complaint, for like many men of his generation, he had little sensitivity to women's needs, not even of the women he loved." This says much in very few words.

Winkler, like the subject of this biography, received his undergraduate degree from Harvard. Unlike FDR, Winkler went on for a Ph.D. in history from Yale. Now he is Distinguished Professor of History at Miami University in Ohio. In addition to co-authoring several textbooks on American history, Winkler has written important books on the Cold War, on the cultural impact of the atom bomb, on the home front during World War II and on the Office of War Information. The present book is the finest concise account of an American whose greatness, however controversial, is indisputable.

MARK C. CARNES

Author's Preface

This is a book I have wanted to write for my entire academic career. I first became interested in Franklin D. Roosevelt in a graduate seminar, taught by John Morton Blum, at Yale University, and found myself increasingly intrigued with the New Deal and World War II years. I was also impressed with a number of volumes in the Library of American Biography series, notably Edmund S. Morgan's elegant *The Puritan Dilemma: The Story of John Winthrop* and John Blum's incisive *Woodrow Wilson and the Politics of Morality*. As I published other books, I decided that I too wanted to try my hand at writing a biography, and I approached the publisher of the series a number of times over the years with a request to write about FDR. Each time, I was told that the book was under contract, though no volume appeared. Finally, the contract became free, and I had my chance at last.

I appreciate the paid leave of absence from Miami University which gave me the time to write. I am also grateful to the University of Canterbury in Christchurch, New Zealand, for providing me with an academic home in the spring of 2004 as I drafted this book. My colleagues there were invariably warm, friendly, and hospitable, and made it a comfortable—and absolutely beautiful—setting in which to work. I would like to extend a special word of thanks to Maureen Montgomery, in the American Studies program there, for making the necessary arrangements for my stay, helping me get settled, and introducing me to others at the university who became my friends. And I was pleased to have the opportunity to present my conclusions at a History Department seminar toward the end of my stay at the University of Canterbury, and benefited from the observations of those who attended.

I am particularly appreciative of the efforts of colleagues and friends who read the manuscript and offered a variety of suggestions for revisions and editorial changes. David M. Kennedy, whose splendid Pulitzer Prize-winning book *Freedom from Fear: The American People in Depression and War, 1929–1945* provided me with a framework for thinking about the period, went through my own manuscript with care. William E. Leuchtenburg, whose *Franklin D. Roosevelt and the New Deal, 1932–1940* was one of the first accounts of the Great Depression I read and remains one of the very best assessments, even after 40 years, likewise provided me with helpful and telling criticism. Roger Daniels, a long-time friend and first-rate historian of American immigration and ethnicity, who is currently writing his own biography of FDR, saved me from any number of mistakes. John W. Jeffries, a friend from my graduate school days and in the years that followed and an important scholar of the World War II years, provided me with the same kind of perceptive critique he has always offered. And Drew Cayton, a close friend and colleague at Miami University, gave me the benefit of his own superb sense of style in the writing of history and helped me smooth the text in numerous places. I would like to thank the students in my Miami University Senior Seminar on FDR, who began the class by reading my draft and then provided a useful critique as they became immersed in their own research papers.

I am also grateful to critics whose reviews, solicited by Longman, were very helpful. My thanks to Connie Killebrew, The University of Texas at Arlington, George Gerdow, Northeastern Illinois University, Simone Caron, Wake Forest University, Thomas Appleton, Eastern Kentucky University, Lee Annis, Montgomery Collegte-Rockville, Roger Bromert, Southwestern Oklahoma State, Tim Mattimoe, Beaufort County Community College.

And in this project, as in virtually all of my work, I am grateful for the close reading of the manuscript by my sister, Karen Winkler Moulton, a perceptive editor at the *Chronicle of Higher Education*, who has always been my very best editor as well, in addition to being a constant source of personal support.

My thanks go to Martha Beyerlein for her careful copy-editing of this manuscript, with the same attention to detail she has provided me frequently in the past.

I appreciate, too, other kinds of assistance. While writing in New Zealand, I occasionally spoke on the telephone with Charles J. Beard, a roommate from Harvard and later a successful Boston attorney, who was battling the effects of multiple myloma. He had suffered from polio as a child, and had beaten that disease. Now he was fighting an even tougher battle, to which he eventually succumbed. But his cheerful conversations from halfway around the world, in the midst of what was for him a terrible time, helped me reflect on FDR's own struggles with the illness that so powerfully affected his life.

I am, as always, grateful to my wife Sara, who stayed back home to help her parents while I went off to New Zealand to write. It was a difficult period for her, I know, but she remained—and remains—the most important person in my life. And I appreciate the emotional presence of my now-grown children, Jenny and David, who have always been a source of pleasure for me.

Finally, I am dedicating this book to Drew and Mary Cayton and Karl and Karen Schilling, four friends in Oxford, Ohio, who enrich my life in countless ways.

ALLAN M. WINKLER

Prologue

In the spring of 1945, Franklin Delano Roosevelt was worn out. His face was gaunt and, though the public did not know it, he was seriously ill. Sixty-three years old in January, he had just been reelected to an unprecedented fourth term as president of the United States. The most extensive war the world had ever known was not yet over, and he was reluctant to leave the White House before the long-sought victory was finally achieved. But his heart was ailing, despite the apparent exuberance with which he had tackled his final campaign, and close associates knew it was unlikely he would leave office alive. Even so, the same sense of commitment that had served him—and the country—so well in the dark days of depression and war drove him on.

Less than three months after his fourth inauguration, Roosevelt was dead. A massive cerebral hemorrhage struck him down as he relaxed at his cottage in Warm Springs, Georgia, a place he had gone for years to try to recover from the ravages of the polio that had left him unable to walk. "Who the hell is President now?" a young sailor in the Pacific wondered, speaking for millions who equated FDR with the presidency itself. British Prime Minister Winston Churchill, with whom Roosevelt had worked so closely during World War II, later wrote that when he had heard the news about his friend's death, "I felt as if I had been struck a physical blow." Mourners waited for hours as the funeral train bearing FDR's body returned to Washington, D.C. His wife Eleanor thought about "The Lonesome Train," a musical poem about Abraham Lincoln's death, and found people stopping her in the street to tell her how much they missed the president and the way "he used to talk to me about my government."

Like Lincoln, Roosevelt over a period of several years was preoccupied by a war that demanded his constant attention. Like Lincoln, his ability to set priorities helped in large part to account for the ultimate victory. And like Lincoln, Roosevelt aroused strong feelings among the people of the nation. Loved by many, hated by some, he was seldom seen in a neutral light. Working-class voters hailed him as the man who provided relief in the dark days of the Great Depression, when a quarter of the nation was unemployed. Wealthy opponents attacked him for undermining what they felt were the very foundations of the capitalist system.

Friends and foes alike acknowledged that Roosevelt was a paradoxical figure. "I cannot come to grips with him!" Harold Ickes, long-serving secretary of the interior, declared. Roosevelt could project a disarming warmth that made people listening to his fireside chats or other speeches believe that he was talking directly to each and every one of them. Yet there was, at the same time, a distance Eleanor once called an "innate kind of reticence" that sometimes left even those closest to him unsure of his intentions. His ability to persuade, despite his own personal reserve, kept the country on course during hard times. In the process, FDR managed to infuriate some subordinates but still retain their affection. After being fired as head of the Department of Commerce in 1945, Jesse Jones publicly called Roosevelt a hypocrite without character, then observed wryly, "You just can't help liking that fellow."

Attacked as a radical by his critics, Roosevelt was committed to the survival of the capitalist state but was never afraid to experiment with change. A pragmatic progressive, committed to the reform sentiments prevailing in early twentieth-century America, he embraced ideas wherever he found them, whether or not they were his own. For he had, in Supreme Court Justice Oliver Wendell Holmes, Jr.'s famous phrase, "a second-class intellect—but a first-class temperament" and understood the need for action to revive the faltering economic order. He could be frustratingly stubborn, once telling Admiral William Leahy during World War II, "I am a pig-headed Dutchman, and you can't change my mind." Yet on other occasions, he was willing to try first one approach, then another, until he found one that worked.

The complexities of Roosevelt's life illustrate many of the complexities of his generation. Raised in a wealthy and influential nineteenth-century family, he had to adjust to tumultuous change as progressives in both political parties demanded—and implemented—social, political, and economic reforms in the early years of the twentieth century, then had to struggle to comprehend and combat catastrophe as a devastating depression rocked the nation as never before. Likewise, Roosevelt's own limitations reflect the limitations of American society in the mid-twentieth century. FDR's unwillingness to embrace the arguments of English economist John Maynard Keynes in the 1930s impeded efforts to try the kind of deficit spending that might have ended the Great Depression sooner, and instead led him to follow a sometimes haphazard approach to keep the nation from falling apart. His single-minded pursuit of victory during World War II occasionally caused him to ignore important values, as when he approved the internment of approximately 120,000 Japanese Americans in the United States, or failed to authorize the entrance of European Jews desperately hoping to come to the United States to escape the horrors of the Holocaust.

Yet Roosevelt's influential legacy lives on. In his first two presidential terms, he embraced the progressive principle—and made it national policy—that the government would help those who could not help themselves. For all of his experimentation with various recovery policies, he was committed to the need for the government to guarantee a measure of security for all Americans, and not just those of means. In his third term, and in the fragment of his fourth before he died, he defended that government and its core values in a ferocious military conflict. He put together a new Democratic coalition that dominated American politics for the next 40 years. He used radio in a remarkable way that changed forever the relationship of politicians with the media. He encouraged a revolution in constitutional interpretation that led the once recalcitrant Supreme Court to accept the process of social reform. And he restored confidence in the hopes and dreams of millions of ordinary Americans. All subsequent presidents—Democrats and Republicans both—have had to deal with his legacy.

1

The Roosevelts of Hyde Park

Franklin Roosevelt was part of the old and established American aristocracy. On his father's side, he came from a family of Dutch descent that had been in the New York area for seven generations. Claes Martenszen Van Rosenvelt arrived first in what was then called Nieuw Amsterdam in 1650 and made the New World his home. On his mother's side, FDR's Huguenot—French Protestant—lineage was equally long. Philippe de la Noye landed in Plymouth, Massachusetts, in 1621, and in time his descendants too ended up in New York.

The Roosevelts prospered by trading in real estate, dry goods, and West Indian sugar. In the eighteenth century, Isaac, a wealthy sugar refiner, voted for independence in the New York Assembly, then fled the city when the British took control. He moved for a while north up the Hudson River to Dutchess County, where the family established its home in the early nineteenth century. Here, not far from Sleepy Hollow, popularized by Washington Irving's stories of Ichabod Crane and Rip Van Winkle, the Roosevelts flourished. They were not the first residents—the Schuylers and Van Rensselaers preceded them—nor were they the wealthiest—the Astors and Vanderbilts were far more well-to-do—but they were comfortably part of the upper crust.

Franklin's father, James, grew up along the Hudson. After graduating from Union College and the Harvard Law School, he worked in a distinguished law firm in New York and moved into the business world as well. He became a director of the Consolidated Coal Company, then general manager of the Cumberland and Pennsylvania Railway. His investment in those enterprises was profitable and allowed him to live the life of a country squire he loved. In 1865, when his home burned down, he bought a modest estate at Crum Elbow in the town of Hyde Park, on the banks of the Hudson, which he named Springwood. Starting with a little more than 100 acres, he expanded his holdings until the entire estate extended over 1,000 acres.

At his home in Hyde Park, James lived the genteel life favored by members of his class. He planted trees, harvested apples and hay, and operated his farm at a profit. An accomplished horseman, he bred trotters and amassed a collection of horse-drawn buggies. He also enjoyed skating, iceboating, sailing, and fishing.

At the same time, his sense of responsibility led him to become a local civic leader. In 1871, he was elected town supervisor, but thereafter declined other requests to run for political office at either the state or national level. Instead, he served on the board of managers of the Hudson River State Hospital and on the Hyde Park school board, where he helped build a new two-story school in the village. Baptized in the Dutch Reformed Church, he became an Episcopalian, his wife's religion and the faith favored by his social set, and was a vestryman and warden at St. James Church.

But he was not always in Hyde Park. Often he, his wife Rebecca, and their only child, also named James but nicknamed "Rosy," were away, traveling in Europe, visiting spas in Germany, shooting grouse in Scotland. On one occasion, while in London, the Roosevelts stopped to visit James Buchanan, the American minister, who asked James to serve as his secretary until the arrival of new embassy personnel. In the summer, they frequently went to Campobello, a Canadian island in the Bay of Fundy, near the Maine border. They liked hiking around the island or sailing in the ocean, surrounded by the sea air and the sound of seabirds along the shore.

Though most of his friends and neighbors were Republicans, James was a Democrat. Many of the members of the social elite had been Democrats prior to the Civil War, but drifted into the Republican Party as it began to promote big business and industry during Reconstruction. James agreed with most of his friends' inclinations on the issues of the day—support of sound money, which meant gold rather than silver, and opposition to inflation demanded by southern and western farmers—but opted for the Democratic Party, perhaps because of his friendship with James Buchanan, who became president several years after James had worked for him at the embassy in London. He was able to be a Democrat and still retain his aristocratic values; his father-in-law once remarked he was "the first person who made me realize that a Democrat can be a gentleman."

Living the life of a man of means, James was dignified and distinguished, comfortable and content. He never wanted for anything and could afford to indulge his tastes and those of his family. He traveled in his own railroad car and not with the ordinary folk who scrambled to find seats on the train. He knew his place in society. His mutton-chop whiskers—sideburns in the contemporary style—gave him the appearance of a gentleman.

His life changed with Rebecca's death in 1876. Continuing his various business and civic ventures as a widower, James maintained an active social life and was soon attracted to the daughter of Warren Delano, a business acquaintance of many years and part of the same social set. The Delanos, like the Roosevelts, had prospered in America, making a fortune in the nineteenth-century opium trade with China, but were now involved in more respectable pursuits. Sara, nicknamed Sallie, had spent part of her early years in Europe, living with her family in France and attending finishing school in Germany, and had also traveled in the Far East. She was strong-willed, but eventually succumbed to her father's wishes and broke off an infatuation with Stanford White, soon to become a highly acclaimed—and controversial—architect, and kept company with James instead. She found him "straight and honorable, just and kind, an upstanding American," and married him in the autumn of 1880. He was 52 years old at the time; she was 26.

On January 30, 1882, Sara gave birth to her only child, Franklin Delano Roosevelt. She had a long and difficult labor, compounded by the doctor's administration of chloroform, which left her unconscious and the newborn baby limp, blue, and unable to breathe. Revived by mouth-to-mouth resuscitation, Franklin quickly flourished. As he was about to go to bed, James recorded in his wife's diary, "At quarter to nine my Sallie had a splendid large baby boy. He weighs 10 lbs., without clothes."

Franklin grew up in secure surroundings. His older brother Rosy was already 28 when Franklin was born and living his own life. Franklin, as a result, had the undivided attention of his parents who lavished attention on him and carefully controlled his upbringing. Sara, in particular, departed from the expectations of the day for a member of her social class by insisting on being intimately involved in every phase of her son's upbringing, taking full responsibility for feeding, changing, and washing him herself, rather than relegating those chores to someone else. There were nannies and governesses, to be sure, but Sara was in charge and did much of the caregiving herself.

She kept Franklin in curls, skirts, and velvet suits as he grew older, until he finally rebelled and insisted on cutting his hair and wearing other, more acceptable clothes. Sara also rigidly prescribed the patterns of her son's daily life. He got up at 7 A.M. and went to bed at 8 P.M., did lessons with tutors at home, and was supervised during recreational time. Because he did not go to school until the age of 14, he had little contact with young people his own age. The extensive amount of time he spent with adults gave him a certain sophistication and sensitivity to their problems, but also made the transition more difficult when he finally went away to boarding school.

In his studies at home, Franklin got a heavy dose of literature and history. He learned—reluctantly—to play the piano, but was happier when his mother introduced him to stamp collecting. She had begun a collection at the age of 5, then passed it on to her brother, who in turn gave it to Franklin when he turned 10. He continued to expand his collection as an adult, even in the White House, and it was one of the passions of his life. Eventually, he had more than a million stamps in 150 albums.

James likewise played an important role in his son's life. He taught him to ride at the age of 4; Franklin had his own pony as a small boy and his own riding horse when he was older. James saw to it that Franklin learned how to swim and skate, and made sure that he could handle both a sailboat and an iceboat as a boy. He taught him to shoot a gun when he was 11, and counseled him never to kill any animal needlessly. Franklin, who became interested in birds, first collected eggs, then nests, and finally birds that he shot and had stuffed. He became an avid ornithologist, keeping long lists of birds sighted at Hyde Park and elsewhere.

Dogs were an important part of Franklin's life as a boy and continued to provide companionship when he was president. When his uncle gave him an Irish setter, his parents refused to let him keep the dog without a commitment to take full responsibility for its care. Franklin fed the dog every morning and evening, and Marksman accompanied him on all hikes and rides.

The sea was perhaps Franklin's most abiding passion. Not only did he enjoy swimming and sailing, but he collected books and prints about nautical life. He read Alfred Thayer Mahan's important book *The Influence of Sea Power on History* and later corresponded with the admiral himself. By the end of his life, he had in his library more than 2,000 books about naval history and 1,200 prints of boats, along with about 200 models of fully rigged ships.

Just as he had done during his first marriage, James traveled with Sara and Franklin. Some of the trips were local, as when the family spent the winter of 1887 in Washington, D.C. On one occasion, James took his son to meet President Grover Cleveland—a Democrat—in the White House. "My little man," Cleveland said, putting his hand on the 5-year-old's head, "I am making a strange wish for you. It is that you may never be president of the United States." Often, though, the family visited Europe, and Franklin went back and forth across the Atlantic numerous times in his youth. In 1896, when he was 14, his parents permitted him to bicycle with a tutor through the Black Forest in Germany, where he had more autonomy than ever before.

All in all, Franklin enjoyed a happy and easy childhood. He was close to his father, whom he called "Popsy," even after a heart attack in 1890 prevented James from actively participating in sports with his son. Franklin learned to live under his mother's watchful eye, while still carving out a sphere of independence for himself. He became skillful at accepting her authority while still preserving a measure of his own personal space, and never seemed bothered by her efforts at control. "In thinking back to my earliest days," he wrote many years later, "I am impressed by the peacefulness and regularity of things both in respect to places and people."

At the age of 14, Franklin's parents decided it was finally time to send him away to school. Reluctantly they knew, in Sara's words, that he needed to venture "out into the world whose boundaries were not limited by the barriers the very intensity of our devotion had imposed." They chose Groton School, about 40 miles northwest of Boston, then the most exclusive private academy in the country. Patterned after such British preparatory schools as Eton, Groton was founded and run by the Reverend Endicott Peabody, a dominating man who inspired fear but also affection in his students. Accepting only boys, and those from a narrow social circle, Groton sought to mold them into Christian gentlemen with a sense of responsibility to both their class and their country. Sara and James wanted that education for their son, but still found the transition painful. "It is hard to leave our darling boy," Sara confided to her diary. "James and I both feel this parting very much."

Franklin joined a class of boys who had already been at the school for two years, and had to adjust quickly to the rigid social and academic patterns. Accustomed to a large, comfortable bedroom at home, he now found himself living in a tiny 6-by-10-foot cubicle with little privacy. The walls were only 7 feet high, and above them was open space all the way to the ceiling, so students could hear what was going on in other cubicles down the hall. There was no door, only a curtain to close off the cubicle from the corridor. The room contained only the bare necessities—a rug, a dresser, a table, a chair, and a hard, narrow bed. The day began at 7 A.M., with a cold shower in the bathroom down the hall, followed by breakfast, chapel, and then classes that started at 8:30 A.M. The curriculum was classical, with a heavy focus on Latin and Greek. Other languages were important as well, and Franklin was fortunate that he could already speak French and German, as a result of his travels abroad. "Dear Mommerr and Popperr," he wrote to his parents in his first letter home, "I am getting on finely, both mentally and physically."

Academically, Franklin did well enough. In the first report sent home to his parents, his grades averaged 7.79 out of a possible 10, with his highest scores for punctuality and neatness. Of the young man who was fourth in his class of 19, the rector wrote, "Very Good. He strikes me as an intelligent & faithful scholar & a good boy." At the end of his stay at Groton, Franklin won the Latin Prize.

Students were expected to participate in extracurricular activities. At his father's insistence, Franklin first tried boxing, but his slight build proved a handicap, and he ended up as manager of the baseball team instead. He also sang in the choir, debated, and took part in other public-speaking activities, giving his first speech on his father's unsuccessful efforts to help build a canal connecting the Atlantic and Pacific Oceans in Nicaragua. He joined the Groton Missionary Society, assisting an elderly African-American woman with household and garden chores and spending a couple of two-week terms at the society's summer camp for poor children in New Hampshire.

As a result of his upbringing, Franklin was well-behaved, and managed to get on well with both the faculty and his fellow students, though some of his classmates found his behavior affected and excessively self-assured. Accustomed to being the center of attention, he sometimes seemed aloof and argumentative. It was something of a relief for him when he got his first black mark for talking during class. "I was very glad I got it," he wrote to his parents, "as I was thought to have no school spirit."

When war with Spain broke out in 1898, the 16-year-old Franklin and a friend talked about running away from school and joining the Navy. They made arrangements to be smuggled away from Groton in the horse-drawn cart of a man selling pastries and pies at the school, but when the designated day arrived, they found themselves confined to the infirmary with scarlet fever instead.

Groton was important to Franklin, and he made the most of his time there. On his final grade report, the rector wrote, "He has been a thoroughly faithful scholar & a most satisfactory member of this school throughout his course. I part with Franklin with reluctance." Many years later, Reverend Peabody reflected on those years: "There has been a good deal written about Franklin Roosevelt when he was a boy at Groton, more than I should have thought justified by the impression that he left at the school. He was a quiet, satisfactory boy of more than ordinary intelligence, taking a good position in his Form but not brilliant. Athletically, he was rather too slight for success. We all liked him." For his part, Franklin wrote to Peabody in 1940, "More than forty years ago, you said in a sermon in the old Chapel, something about not losing boyhood ideals in later life. Those were Groton ideals—taught by you—I try not to forget—and your words are still with me and with the hundreds of others of 'us boys.'"

In 1900, Franklin moved on to Harvard University, not far from Groton, and an equally appropriate venue for a member of his social set. Initially, he had wanted to go to the United States Naval Academy at Annapolis, but bowed to his father's wishes that he attend Harvard. There, he chose to live not in Harvard Yard with most of the other students, but in one of the private dormitories known as the Gold Coast on Mount Auburn Street in Cambridge. He and a Groton classmate found a spacious suite, far more luxurious than what the prep school had provided, and he took most of his meals not in the new Harvard Union, where most students ate, but elsewhere with old Groton friends.

In college, Franklin was an adequate student. He listened to lectures given by some of the leading intellectuals in the country—including historian Frederick Jackson Turner, economist William Z. Ripley, and philosopher Josiah Royce—and did enough work to get by. With his Groton preparation standing him in good stead, he was able to fulfill the requirements for his B.A. degree in three years, though his enjoyment of both extracurricular activities and social life led him to stay at Harvard for a fourth year rather than leave early.

At Harvard, Franklin sought to follow in the footsteps of his famous fifth cousin Theodore, hero of the Cuban campaign in the Spanish American War in 1898 and president of the United States in the early years of the twentieth century. In the summer of 1897, Franklin had visited Theodore and his family at Sagamore Hill on Long Island in New York, and he looked up to the exuberant politician with the wide toothy grin. He had been especially proud of his association with his flamboyant cousin when Theodore spoke at Groton about his experience as head of the New York City Board of Police Commissioners. At Harvard, Franklin adopted some of his cousin's mannerisms, wearing pince-nez—spectacles without side pieces hooking over his ears—and sprinkling his speech with TR's favorite words, such as "bully" and "*delighted*," with a stress on the first syllable. Some of the young women in his social circle made fun of his affectations and called him "the featherduster."

His real passion at Harvard was the *Crimson*, the student newspaper. Joining the staff in his first year, he hoped that he would be chosen as one of the few to move up and become an editor. Spending up to six hours a day on the daily paper, he came up with a notable scoop when he was the first to learn that his cousin Theodore, now the nation's vice president, was coming to the campus for a visit. The four-column *Crimson* headline announcing his lecture drew two thousand students to the 500-seat auditorium and gave Franklin valuable visibility when TR greeted him warmly in front of hundreds of students. In the spring, Franklin became one of five new *Crimson* editors; in the second semester of his third year he became managing editor; and in the first term of his final year, while he was ostensibly taking courses for an M.A. degree he never completed, he became president, or editor-in-chief. His newspaper work served him in good stead, teaching him to meet deadlines, and to work closely and cooperatively with the sometimes irascible commercial printers who produced the paper. His successor as president of the *Crimson* gave him credit for having "liked people and having made them instinctively like him . . . In his geniality there was a kind of frictionless command."

His one major disappointment at Harvard was his rejection for membership in the most exclusive social club, Porcellian. His father James was an honorary member, and his cousin Theodore had been selected during his college days. Franklin lost his chance when he was blackballed by at least one member in the secret election process. Eleanor later claimed that it gave him an "inferiority complex," and Franklin himself was to call the rejection "one of the great disappointments of my life." He was elected to the somewhat less prestigious Fly Club and also to the larger but still elite Hasty Pudding Society.

Largely because of his cousin Theodore's influence and impact, he joined the Harvard Republican Club and voted for TR in 1904. But later, when he surveyed his own political prospects, he found himself more sympathetic to the Democratic Party and its progressive goals, and he ended up following his father's example and remained a

Democrat for the rest of his life. Even when the Republican TR, having left the presidency in 1909, tried to make a comeback in 1912, Franklin, now actively involved in Democratic politics, provided vigorous support for the ultimately successful Woodrow Wilson.

While at Harvard, Franklin still had to deal with family issues. His father suffered another heart attack, then still another, and finally died in December 1900. Franklin was by his side, and stayed with his mother for a month before returning to college. Lonely at Hyde Park, Sara decided to live in Boston during the winters of 1902 and 1903 to be closer to her son. She had friends and relatives in the area, but her real focus was on Franklin. If the attention was sometimes oppressive, it taught him to protect his own independence when necessary.

For he was caught up in a social life his mother knew little about. As he went to the debutante parties and other gatherings required of those in his position, he became increasingly attracted to his fifth cousin Eleanor Roosevelt, daughter of Elliott Roosevelt, Theodore's younger brother, and Elliott's wife Anna. Involvement with Eleanor showed a depth of sensitivity and understanding the glib and dapper Franklin had not revealed before.

Though Eleanor was part of the same social circle, she had not had an easy life. Her father, whom she idolized and once called "the one great love of my life as a child," became addicted first to pain-killing drugs—morphine and laudanum—while recovering from a badly broken ankle, and later to alcohol. After he was sent away by her mother (under pressure from Theodore), Eleanor only saw him rarely. She still loved him and wanted to see him, but felt abandoned when he failed to visit her or, on one occasion, left her with the doorman at a club when he went inside for a drink. Her mother, troubled by headaches, eroded her daughter's self-confidence by making fun of what she felt was Eleanor's serious nature and lack of beauty, calling her "Granny" and telling others, "She is such a funny child, so old-fashioned." Anna died of diphtheria in 1892 when Eleanor was eight, and she was sent to live with her grandmother. "I do not feel she has much chance, poor little soul," remarked Edith Roosevelt, Theodore's wife. Two years later, the debauched Elliott took a fall that knocked him unconscious and led to his death. Eleanor was an orphan, painfully awkward, unhappy, and insecure. Edith, however, saw something there, observing after a visit that while Eleanor "is very plain. . . . the ugly duckling may turn out to be a swan."

She brightened up when sent to study at Allenswood, a French-language school outside London, in Great Britain. In a somewhat austere environment, Eleanor thrived as she studied many of the same classical subjects Franklin had taken, and took an active role in such sports as field hockey. She also found herself drawn to Mlle. Marie Souvestre, the headmistress, who was particularly fond of Eleanor and became both a mentor and a friend. To Eleanor's grandmother, who had enrolled her in the school, Souvestre wrote: "All what you said when she came here of the purity of her heart, the nobleness of her thought has been verified by her conduct among people who were at first perfect strangers to her. . . . She is full of sympathy for all those who live with her and shows an intelligent interest in everything she comes in contact with."

Returning to the United States, Eleanor worked occasionally as a settlement-house volunteer on New York's Lower East Side, helping urban immigrants in their adjustment to American life. But she had not yet dedicated herself to social service and knew she could not ignore the demands of her class. She was going to have to make her debut to society, the elaborate coming-out ritual expected of young women of her station. She dreaded the occasion, noting later that "I knew I was the first girl in my mother's family who was not a belle, and though I [never] acknowledged it to any of them at the time, I was deeply ashamed." In fact, she was quite pretty. Though she was conscious of her prominent teeth and small chin, her eyes sparkled and, even if she was still occasionally awkward, she was willowy with a kind of radiance. She managed, with some difficulty, to get through the first party, and as she attended others, her distant cousin Franklin began to notice her.

Their paths had crossed before. In 1886, when she was two, Eleanor had come with her parents to Hyde Park and played with Franklin, who had carried her around on his back, and there were other occasions when they had been together. On her return from Europe, Eleanor met Franklin again on a train to New York. In the months that followed, they saw more of each other at debutante parties. "Cousin Eleanor has a very good mind," he reported to his mother. Franklin asked Eleanor to lunch and to tea, and later to Hyde Park. In the fall of 1903, he invited her to the Harvard–Yale football game in Cambridge, where he was performing as a cheerleader. Though he was exuberant, Harvard lost by a score of 16–0. The next day, he accompanied Eleanor to Groton, just a few miles away, where she had just enrolled Hall, her younger brother. While walking through the woods, Franklin asked Eleanor to marry him, and she accepted, writing him a letter the next day quoting from a poem titled "A Woman's Shortcomings" by Elizabeth Barrett Browning, that included the lines:

> Unless you can think when the song is done,
> No other is left in the rhythm; ...
> Unless you can swear, "For life, for death!"
> Oh, fear to call it loving!

Now Franklin had to tell his mother. The news took her by surprise, and she was furious. "I don't believe I remember ever hearing him talk about girls," she later wrote. He was too young, she felt, too inexperienced. Worst of all, he had courted Eleanor secretly, in violation of her expectation that she would be involved in all parts of his life. Sara did her best to dissuade him, even taking him and a friend on a cruise to the West Indies to try to get his mind off Eleanor, in the hope that he would break off the engagement, but to no avail.

Eleanor and Franklin were a study in contrasts. He was lighthearted and handsome, with his eyebrows dark and his hair cut short. He enjoyed talking to people and bantering with friends. She was serious and still found it difficult to think of herself as pretty. She was also much more reticent, particularly with people she did not know. But Franklin provided her with what she called "a sense of security which I had never known before," and so she committed herself to him. He, in turn, recognized in Eleanor a depth of feeling and a seriousness of purpose he had not encountered in other people he knew.

When invited to the wedding, Theodore, now president, wrote to Franklin: "I am as fond of Eleanor as if she were my daughter, and I like you, and trust you, and believe in you. . . . May all good fortune attend you both, ever . . . Your affectionate cousin." He came to New York to give the bride away at the wedding, which took place on March 17, 1905, telling Franklin, "There's nothing like keeping the name in the family." Most of the guests at the wedding were more interested in the buoyant president than in the newlyweds.

It was not easy for Eleanor to adjust to married life. She was never fond of sex, finding it, she later told her daughter, an ordeal to be endured. Nor was she comfortable as part of what now became a triangular relationship, for

Sara remained very much a part of their lives. Franklin had chosen to study law at Columbia University in New York, to be closer to Eleanor during their engagement, and they intended to live in the city. After returning from their honeymoon, they moved into a house that Sara had furnished by herself, without consulting Eleanor. It was just three blocks from Sara's own home on East Thirty-sixth Street. A few years later, Sara built the young family another house on East Sixty-fifth Street, with a common vestibule and a door in an adjoining wall between that structure and one she built for herself at the same time. It was hard for Eleanor to find a place to be alone.

Eleanor and Franklin settled into their life together. Franklin completed his required legal courses at Columbia, though he never graduated from law school. On passing the bar exam, which he could take nonetheless, he went to work in 1907 for the firm of Carter, Ledyard, and Milburn on Wall Street, spending most of his time in municipal court work. Eleanor bore one child after another—Anna, James, Franklin, Jr. (who died when just several months old), Elliott, another Franklin, Jr., and finally John. She was not always happy at being "an entirely dependent person," and felt constrained by Sara's presence. When she tried to tell Franklin of her frustrations, he listened but found it hard to understand her complaint, for like many men of his generation, he had little sensitivity to women's needs, not even of the women he loved. In time, Eleanor became more reconciled to her situation, for the family was comfortable and secure, well-off financially, with a bright future ahead.

2

Political and Personal Affairs

Franklin Roosevelt started his career as a lawyer but dreamed of being a politician. Married and settled into domestic life, he and his growing family lived in New York City, under his mother's watchful eye. The Roosevelt name carried a good deal of weight there and had helped him secure his first job. It became even more important as he began to think seriously about involvement in the world of politics and public service. By the time he was 28 years old, he had begun the climb that eventually brought him to the presidency of the United States.

Carter, Ledyard, and Milburn was an old and distinguished law firm. One senior partner owned the house in Buffalo where President William McKinley died after sustaining a gunshot wound and where Theodore Roosevelt took the presidential oath of office, and he was counsel for Standard Oil of New Jersey, one of America's huge corporate trusts. Another senior partner was a friend of J. P. Morgan, the best-known financier in the nation, and he served as counsel for the American Tobacco Company, equally dominant in the industrial sphere. The major focus of Carter, Ledyard, and Milburn was on corporate and admiralty law, and it dedicated itself to finding ways to circumvent the Sherman Anti-Trust Act, passed in

1890, and now being used by Theodore Roosevelt to try to control the country's great conglomerates.

Franklin Roosevelt became a clerk, with no salary for the first year, according to the pattern of the day, as he learned how the firm operated. He worked on none of the important cases; indeed, he confessed to his mother that he was little more than a "full-fledged office boy," doing tedious and boring chores for the partners. He searched for references in the law library, carried deeds to the county clerk's office, and ran other errands. With a sense of self-deprecation, he advertised himself in a joking, handwritten notice as a "counselor at law" specializing in "unpaid bills," chloroforming "small dogs," preparing briefs on "the liquor question," and similar tasks. He was happier when he was given minor cases to argue in municipal court, where he became skillful at the rough and tumble maneuvering of local legal work. Though in most cases he defended large corporate clients faced with petty claims from customers who felt they had been gouged, the courtroom struggles gave him a first sense of how ordinary people lived and worked in a world where they fought against forces beyond their control.

Still, he was bored with his life as a lawyer. He knew he had a predictable future ahead of him if he simply dedicated himself to his work. The way was clear to move up the hierarchy of the firm until he became a wealthy senior partner, able to enjoy the exclusive social clubs to which he already belonged and the hobbies, such as stamp collecting and bird watching, that had delighted him for years. Yet he needed something more. He wanted to be taken seriously, to be considered, in the words of a friend writing later, more than "a harmless bust." One day at the firm, he confided in five of the other law clerks his plans for the future. He wanted to run for political office as soon as he could. He intended to follow in his cousin

Theodore's footsteps, looking toward a seat in the New York State Assembly, then a position as assistant secretary of the navy, and after that, governor of New York. And then, he said, "if you do well enough in that job, you have a good show to be president."

His opportunity soon came. Dutchess County voted largely Republican, but there was still a strong Democratic presence in Poughkeepsie, not far from Hyde Park, and party leaders knew that Franklin, like his father, was a Democrat and would make an attractive candidate. He was handsome, outgoing, wealthy, and possessed an impressive family name. In early 1910, District Attorney John E. Mack came to New York to see Roosevelt on a business matter, and ended up offering him the nomination for a soon-to-be-vacated state assembly seat from Poughkeepsie.

The Democratic incumbent, however, decided he wanted to remain in the assembly after all. Mack tried to mollify Roosevelt by offering him the nomination to the state senate instead. The nomination was easy enough to arrange. Election to the senate was going to be considerably more difficult, he acknowledged, perhaps even impossible, in the heavily Republican district.

As Roosevelt pondered whether or not to run, he got mixed messages from those whose advice he sought. Lewis Cass Ledyard, his boss at the law firm, felt that he was throwing away a promising legal career. His ebullient cousin Theodore, despite his Republican affiliation, was more positive, telling his sister that "Franklin should go into politics without the least regard as to where I speak or don't speak." Roosevelt's immediate family was likewise divided. His mother was uncomfortable at the thought of her son having to spend so much time in close contact with the masses and still wanted him to lead the leisurely life his father had enjoyed. Only Eleanor, with her own sense of public service, encouraged him to enter politics.

One problem was that entering politics in New York meant dealing with Tammany Hall, the New York City Democratic political machine. Active since the mid-nineteenth century, it had an epic reputation for corruption and the unbridled use of power. The Tweed Ring, named for Boss William Marcy Tweed, stole million of dollars from public-works projects, and the organization remained intact even after Tweed was toppled from his leadership position. Relying on an immigrant base, it provided services in return for votes and so maintained its power. Politics, as Theodore Roosevelt understood, was a difficult profession for men of standing.

Roosevelt nonetheless accepted the nomination and plunged into the campaign. He knew he had hard work ahead of him, for he was up against a Republican incumbent in a district covering three counties that had sent only one Democrat to the state senate since 1856. The odds, Mack told him, were five to one against his election. Roosevelt made a splash by renting a topless red Maxwell touring car to take him around the district. It was a bold and visible gesture in the early days of the automobile that appealed to voters, even if it was difficult traveling on bad roads in a vehicle that frequently broke down. On one occasion, Roosevelt ended up in a small town and bought drinks for all customers at a local bar, only to learn too late that he had strayed across the state line and was in Connecticut.

Though he was energetic and exuberant, he was hardly a compelling orator. Eleanor, home with young children, did not travel with him regularly, and when she saw him once in Poughkeepsie, she found him "high-strung, and at times nervous." He sometimes paused for so long after making a point that she wondered if he had lost his train of thought and was going to be able to go on. Gradually, he became more relaxed and self-assured, able to joke about himself in front of his audiences. After an introduction, he learned how to begin by saying, "I'm not Teddy." When the crowd laughed, he continued, "A little shaver said to me the other day that he knew I wasn't Teddy—I asked him 'why' and he replied: 'Because you don't show your teeth.'"

Roosevelt targeted particular voters as he campaigned. Paying little attention to Democratic strongholds in cities like Poughkeepsie, he concentrated on rural farmers, who traditionally voted Republican. Because of his interest in farming, nurtured on the family estate, he understood their needs and had an instinctive sense of how to appeal to them. Without addressing specific problems, he assured them he understood their longstanding economic difficulties, which he blamed on the control of political bosses at both the state and national level. Rain toward the end of the campaign was helpful, as farmers could not work, and so turned out to hear him as he continued to drive from one town to another.

On election day, Roosevelt won a seat in the state senate by a vote of 15,708 to 14,568, a margin of 1,140 votes that was double that of the victorious candidate for governor in his district. Democrats also regained control of both houses of the New York legislature. Though this was a party victory, Roosevelt could also view it as a personal triumph.

Now he had to work with Tammany Hall. Moving to Albany, Roosevelt almost immediately found himself involved in a political fight with Tammany Boss Charles F. Murphy, who proposed William F. Sheehan, a wealthy businessman, for the United States Senate. In an age before the direct election of senators, each state legislature had the power of choice, and the Democrats now had the chance to make the selection. Tammany's power rested on its use of patronage, and Murphy needed to reward his strongest supporters, who could help maintain the organization's strength. But a young group of insurgents that included Roosevelt, uncomfortable with the choice of Sheehan, rebelled. They voiced the arguments in favor of political reform that were part of the larger progressive movement, boycotted the party caucus, and issued a manifesto proclaiming that "the votes of those who represented the people should not be smothered." Meeting daily in the large and comfortable home Roosevelt had rented near the capitol in Albany, the group, which ranged in number from 10 to 20 men, held out for two-and-a-half months, capitulating only when Sheehan's name was withdrawn, and a compromise candidate, no better than Sheehan, was proposed. Though most observers saw that as a defeat for the insurgents, Roosevelt characteristically sought to portray it in the best possible light. "Two months ago a number of Democrats felt it was our duty to dissent," he told his fellow legislators. "We have followed the dictates of our consciences. . . . I believe that as a result the Democratic party has taken an upward step."

The new legislator supported other causes popular with progressives who sought to reform economic, political, and social abuses in American society. In the late nineteenth and early twentieth centuries, activists in both political parties, working at the local, state, and national levels, demanded regulation of the nation's largest businesses, reform of political structures that permitted corrupt political machines to thrive, and assistance for those living at the lowest level of society who were barely able to eke out a living. Though Roosevelt himself came from a background of privilege, he was developing a sense of empathy for those less fortunate that provided a base for his actions as he moved up the political ladder. In the state senate, Roosevelt came out in favor of a national constitutional amendment providing for the direct election of

U.S. senators, and his resolution passed. After the horrendous fire at the Triangle Shirtwaist Company in New York City in 1911—which killed 146 people, mostly immigrant Jewish and Italian women who were locked in a building without fire escapes to prevent them from taking what the firm considered frivolous breaks—he voted for a bill supported by progressives limiting the number of hours women and children could work to 54 per week, though he did so in absentia. Subsequently, he supported other reform legislation that came out of a commission formed in the aftermath of the fire, which included state senate leader Robert F. Wagner as chairman, State Assemblyman Alfred E. Smith as vice chairman, and labor lobbyist Frances Perkins as chief investigator.

Roosevelt was also interested in issues of conservation. He always looked back to his rural roots in Hyde Park and was pleased to become chairman of the senate's Forest, Fish, and Game Committee. He sought advice from Gifford Pinchot, who had been the nation's chief forester under Theodore Roosevelt, and arranged for Pinchot to lecture in the assembly chamber. But efforts to control logging aroused the opposition of lumber leaders and other businessmen and made a real change in policy difficult to achieve. Roosevelt also sought to limit damage done at power sites, and that effort likewise showed him the strength of the utility companies.

Those efforts helped him look more closely at a variety of ideas percolating during the progressive years. They were articulated by authors such as economist Thorstein Veblen, who pointed to the overwhelming power of the capitalist system, and social philosopher Herbert Croly, who asserted the need for a strong national government as part of what came to be called the New Nationalism, and legal theorist Louis Brandeis, who favored breaking apart the large corporations, in what was termed the New Freedom.

As Roosevelt examined such ideas, he began to formulate his own sense of the need for government to protect the public welfare from private greed. In a speech in Troy in 1912, he pointed to the problems of unbridled individualism and declared, "Conditions of civilization that come with individual freedom are inevitably bound to bring up many questions that mere individual liberty cannot solve." A new social theory was necessary: "I have called this new theory the struggle for the liberty of the community rather than the liberty of the individual." In the event of conflict, "the right of any one individual to work or not as he sees fit, to live to a great extent where and how he sees fit, is not sufficient." Though his ideas were not yet fully developed, FDR had started accepting progressive ideas, making them his own, and defining for himself the role of an activist government that could restrain selfish individualism.

Roosevelt's first term as a legislator was good for Eleanor. She enjoyed living in Albany, where she could escape the control of her strong-willed mother-in-law. She felt that "it was a wife's duty to be interested in whatever interested her husband," and so she began to follow politics more closely, often sitting in the capitol gallery and listening to debates. She made friends with the insurgents who met in her home and observed that "I used to go into the pantry and bring out beer and cheese and crackers, which was a gentle hint that the time had come for everyone to eat, drink, and go home." At the same time, she was beginning to realize that something inside her "craved to be an individual." She helped her husband's career along, even as she began to think about her own needs for the first time.

For Franklin, the first term had mixed results. He was highly visible and, with his famous name, commanded considerable attention. The *New York Times* reported early in his term that he had "the finely chiselled face of a

Roman patrician, only with a ruddier glow of health on it. . . . He is tall and lithe. With his handsome face and his form of supple strength, he could make a fortune on the stage and set the matinee girl's heart throbbing with subtle and happy emotion."

But not everyone in Albany was comfortable with him. He had an ambiguous and increasingly competitive relationship with Al Smith, an immigrant from New York City's Lower East Side who went on to become a major force in the Democratic Party. Robert Wagner, an urban reformer who made his mark in the New York State Senate before moving on to the United States Senate, found the young FDR insufferable, and once commented after a flamboyant gesture, "Senator Roosevelt has made his point. What he wants is a headline in the newspapers. Let us proceed to our business." Frances Perkins, herself wholly committed to social reform, thought Roosevelt was not entirely serious and did not like his histrionic habit of tossing his head arrogantly and saying, "No, no, I won't hear of it!" FDR himself recognized some of his early excesses, and later remarked to Perkins, "You know, I was an awfully mean cuss when I first went into politics."

In 1912, Roosevelt sought reelection to the state senate. He was not on good terms with Tammany Hall, which he viewed as hopelessly corrupt and excessively conservative—the very antithesis of the progressive approach—but he still had to contend with the New York City Democratic leaders, for they had statewide influence. As he began to follow national politics more closely, he was well aware that after four years of the conservative Republican William Howard Taft, the United States needed more vigorous presidential leadership. Considering alternatives, he knew one possibility was his cousin Teddy, four years out of the presidency, who was seeking to return to national politics as leader of the new Progressive (Bull Moose)

Party because he was unable to wrest the Republican nomination from Taft. But Franklin was unwilling to bolt the Democratic Party, and he began to think more seriously about Governor Woodrow Wilson of neighboring New Jersey. Wilson had recently pushed through a number of progressive measures reforming state electoral practices, giving a commission the power to set utility rates, and providing for workmen's compensation. Roosevelt visited Wilson and soon after began helping organize a movement in New York for Wilson as president.

Roosevelt attended the Democratic national convention in Baltimore, though not as an official member of the New York delegation. He enjoyed the parading and endless balloting, though Eleanor, who accompanied him, "understood little or nothing of what was going on" and was "appalled" by the "senseless" circus-like demonstrations. She left the convention early, sure she would not be missed. When Wilson finally won the nomination on the forty-sixth ballot, Roosevelt sent her a telegram reading: "WILSON NOMINATED THIS AFTERNOON ALL MY PLANS VAGUE STOP SPLENDID TRIUMPH."

Now he had to secure his own nomination to keep his state senate seat. Though the New York Democratic Party punished many of the insurgents for their struggle with the Tammany-dominated leadership, Roosevelt was renominated. Then he fell ill with typhoid fever and was bedridden for weeks, at just the time he should have been campaigning.

Roosevelt knew he needed help, and he turned to Louis McHenry Howe, a newspaper reporter he had met in Albany. Howe was about five feet tall and weighed around a hundred pounds. He had suffered from asthma, bronchitis, and a heart murmur as a child, but that did not stop him from smoking all the time. He wore rumpled clothes that were often dirty, and looked like a "medieval gnome," in the words of a fellow reporter. He called himself "one of the four ugliest men, if what is left of me can be dignified by the name of man, in the State of New York." Sara Roosevelt could not stand him, calling him "that dirty little man," and initially Eleanor agreed. But Howe was passionately interested in politics, knew how to operate in the political realm, and was looking for a candidate with whom he could work. He had recognized Roosevelt's appeal as he watched him in Albany and, after the Democratic convention, sent him a letter that began, "Beloved and Revered Future President." When the ailing Roosevelt asked his wife to send for Howe, the reporter came at once.

Howe orchestrated Roosevelt's reelection campaign. He decided to follow the basic approach Roosevelt had used in 1910, focusing on rural residents who usually voted Republican. He tried to steer clear of provoking a fight with Tammany over the issue of boss politics, and he likewise was careful to secure labor support without provoking farmers, who felt their interests were different from those of workers. He put together a strong organization that could function in Roosevelt's absence, and he prepared full-page advertisements in county newspapers. On election day, Roosevelt was reelected by a larger margin than when he had run two years before and outpolled both Wilson and the Democratic gubernatorial candidate in his district.

Delighted with his victory, Roosevelt now looked ahead to the next step. He knew that he faced difficulties in the senate and would have to conduct himself carefully to avoid further antagonizing the Democratic leadership. At the same time, he was thinking about alternatives for his own advancement. In early 1913, he went to New Jersey to confer with President-elect Wilson. He was offered first the post of assistant secretary of the treasury and then that of collector of the port of New York, but he declined both, thinking all the while about the position his cousin Theodore had held years before. On inauguration day in March, he received an offer to be assistant secretary of the navy, and he accepted it immediately. Many of the Democrats in Albany were happy to see him go. Republican Senator Elihu Root, who had served as secretary of state under TR, was wary of the appointment. "Whenever a Roosevelt rides," he said, "he wishes to ride in front."

Roosevelt, who had long loved the sea, was delighted with the navy position. Moving into his new office and sitting at Theodore Roosevelt's old desk, he wrote exuberantly to his wife: "The delightful significance of it all is just beginning to dawn on me." He was just 32 years old, a little older than TR when he had held the post, but still on course for the career he coveted. As second in command of a force of 269 ships and 65,000 men, he was entitled to a 17-gun salute whenever he boarded a battleship (an admiral received only a 13-gun salvo). Eleanor, for her part, never thought "to question where we were to go or what we were to do or how we were to do it." With an entourage of children, servants, nurse, and governess, she moved to Washington, into a house near the Capitol.

The secretary of the navy—Roosevelt's boss—was Josephus Daniels, an old-fashioned newspaperman from North Carolina who had served as director of publicity in Wilson's campaign for the presidency. He knew far less about the sea than Roosevelt, but he knew how Washington worked, and he was determined to modernize the outmoded navy and make sure it was in fighting shape.

He gave Roosevelt responsibility for the navy's business affairs. In his relations with businessmen, FDR sought to eliminate collusive bidding, particularly on the part of coal and steel companies. In his contacts with labor leaders, he tried to persuade them that he understood their problems, and he was proud of the fact that he managed to avoid crippling strikes in U.S. Navy yards. He also tried to smooth relations among Daniels and the top navy brass who did not take the unassuming secretary seriously.

With his nautical background and sense that he knew more about the sea than his superior, who considered military ceremony "flummery," Roosevelt exhibited an unattractive arrogance at the start. Once, when Daniels was away, FDR joked that a Roosevelt was again in charge, referring back to the time when TR had been temporarily in charge of the Navy Department in 1898 and had ordered Commodore George Dewey to ready an attack on the Spanish fleet in Manila Bay in the Philippines. Eleanor, more courteous and less self-assured than her husband, found that comment "horrid." Roosevelt also called Daniels "the funniest looking hillbilly I had ever seen" and was fond of imitating him in front of friends when the secretary was not around. Such behavior led Franklin Lane, secretary of the interior, to confront Roosevelt and tell him he ought to be ashamed of himself. If he could not be loyal to Daniels, Lane said, then he should resign. Slowly, Roosevelt began to appreciate both Daniels' methods and his vision for the navy, and to realize that he had a good deal to learn from his elder chief.

While working at his navy job, Roosevelt kept in close touch with groups that could prove useful in his political career. Grateful to Howe for his role in the 1912 campaign, he brought the wizened reporter with him to Washington as his personal secretary. Navy officials were mortified by Howe's appearance, and one captain declared that if Howe ever boarded his ship, the crew would immediately "take him up on the foc'sle, strip him and scrub him down with sand and canvas." But Howe played a crucial role in helping Roosevelt reach out to labor leaders, suggesting projects he might consider, providing material for speeches, and looking for opportunities for his boss's political advancement.

Roosevelt was an attractive presence in Washington. Looking back, Daniels recalled, "How young and debonair, striding and strong he had been!" Bainbridge Colby, who served later in Wilson's presidency as secretary of state, called Roosevelt "the handsomest and most attractive man in Washington." Eleanor did her part to advance her husband's career in expected ways, calling on the wives of Supreme Court justices, leaders of Congress, members of the cabinet, and diplomats, as well as giving and going to parties. At evening gatherings, she often sat quietly knitting, listening to what was going on and learning about the issues of the day. The Roosevelts were clearly people in demand. Even so, some doubts about FDR's seriousness of purpose persisted. His friend Assistant Secretary of State William Phillips once observed, "He was likable and attractive, but not a heavyweight, brilliant but not particularly steady in his views. He could charm anybody but lacked greatness. . . . He was always amusing, always the life of the party, but he did not seem fully mature."

Roosevelt made one potentially damaging political miscalculation in his hurry to move ahead. In 1914, without consulting Howe, he decided at the last minute to seek the Democratic nomination from New York for the United States Senate. Assuming mistakenly that he had Wilson's support, he ran a lackluster campaign against the organization candidate who was now serving as Wilson's ambassador to Germany. Roosevelt never had a chance, and he was badly beaten in the primary. He shook off the defeat easily, however, and suffered no irreparable harm. Indeed, he learned the important lesson that he needed both Tammany support and the assistance of upstate reformers to have a chance for political success in the future.

The outbreak of war in Europe in 1914 made Roosevelt's job in the Navy Department all the more important.

The assassination in the Balkans of the Archduke Franz Ferdinand, heir to the Austro-Hungarian throne, started a war that quickly engulfed Europe and then much of the world. Two alliances—one consisting of Great Britain, France, and Russia, the other of Germany, Austria-Hungary, and Turkey—fought against one another in what became a deadly and devastating conflict. Urging the United States to "be neutral in fact as well as in name . . . impartial in thought as well as in action," Wilson hoped to keep the United States out of the war while playing the role of impartial mediator.

Daniels agreed with the president. Like his cabinet colleague, Secretary of State William Jennings Bryan, he clung to a belief in isolationism out of a fear that militaristic entanglement in the quarrels of foreign nations could compromise America's special destiny. Roosevelt felt otherwise. Following in the tradition of TR, he believed that war was sometimes necessary to protect the United States and to ensure that the nation was prepared. He pushed hard to persuade his navy boss to take what he felt were essential steps to preserve American safety, and sometimes even acted on his own. "I have gone ahead and pulled the trigger myself," he remarked on one occasion. "I suppose the bullet may bounce back on me." Fortunately for him, Daniels was fond of his assistant secretary and chose not to challenge what he might have considered insubordination.

Unrestricted German submarine warfare brought a change in policy. In particular, the sinking of the British passenger liner *Luisitania* in mid-1915—with the loss of 1,195 lives, 128 of them Americans—horrified Wilson and led him to accept the need for preparedness. Seeking a second term in 1916, he ran under the slogan "He kept us out of war," while still supporting preparation with the acknowledgment that any "little German lieutenant can put us into war at any time by some calculated outrage." When the Germans revived submarine attacks in 1917, after having backed off for a time, the president reluctantly asked Congress for a declaration of war. The United States was now inextricably involved.

Roosevelt wanted to enlist. Theodore Roosevelt had left the Navy Department to lead the Rough Riders in the Spanish-American War in 1898, and his nephew now wanted to be involved in the fighting in a similar way. Wilson told Daniels in no uncertain terms that Roosevelt should remain in the Navy Department. "Neither you nor I nor Franklin Roosevelt has the right to select the place of service to which our country has assigned us," he said. "Tell the young man to stay where he is." When Roosevelt went to see the president himself to seek permission to resign and fight, he received the same answer.

Roosevelt finally got the chance to go abroad. In 1918, traveling by destroyer, he went to England where he met Prime Minister David Lloyd George and to France where he spoke with Premier Georges Clemenceau. He also sought to get as close to the fighting as he could on the Continent, visiting Chateau-Thierry, Belleau Wood, and Verdun, moving to within a mile of enemy lines, where he could see pockmarked earth, makeshift crosses, and discarded equipment, and hear guns going off. It was his first view of war—of "the darkness and constant fighting without rest or sleep"—and he never forgot it. He made another trip to Europe in 1919, this time with Eleanor, to dismantle naval operations as the war came to an end, and returned with Wilson and his wife at the end of the Peace Conference at Versailles.

In 1920, Roosevelt resigned his position as assistant secretary of the navy to run for the vice presidency of the United States on a ticket with presidential candidate James M. Cox. He knew the nation was disillusioned with the war, and with the unsuccessful attempt on the part of Wilson to get the United States to sign the Treaty of Versailles and join the fledgling League of Nations. He recognized that the Democrats had little chance of maintaining control of the White House, but running for national office gave him a chance to gain important exposure and make new political contacts as he looked ahead. Along with Eleanor and Louis Howe, he traveled by train across the country as part of the campaign. Eleanor, who had been uncomfortable with Howe when she first met him, listened to him for hours and found him becoming one of her close friends. The election ended as expected. Warren G. Harding won the presidency as the Republicans swept into office, and the nation began to enjoy the unprecedented prosperity of the 1920s. For the first time in a decade, Roosevelt was a private citizen again.

During this period, Roosevelt went through two crises, one emotional, one physical. While in Washington, Eleanor bore her last two children and, never having enjoyed sex, practiced birth control by abstinence, which included moving into a separate bedroom. Meanwhile, given her increasing duties, in 1914 she hired a young woman named Lucy Mercer to be her social secretary. Lucy helped sort out Eleanor's correspondence and plan her schedule, and she soon became a personal and family friend. Often she ate with the Roosevelts, and sometimes accompanied Franklin to dinners when Eleanor could not go. She was lively and attractive and, over time, she and Franklin entered into an intimate relationship. Despite their efforts at discretion, some people in Washington knew what was going on. Alice Roosevelt Longworth, TR's outspoken daughter, invited Franklin—and Lucy— to dinner when Eleanor was out of town. "He deserved a good time," she said tartly. "He was married to Eleanor." While continuing to assist Eleanor, Lucy enlisted in the navy and became a secretary in the Navy Department, working near FDR. Eleanor was increasingly suspicious about the relationship, as were others in Washington, and, later that year, Daniels ended Lucy's assignment at the Navy Department.

In 1918, Franklin returned from his first trip to Europe ill with pneumonia. He went to his mother's house in New York to recuperate, and Eleanor came up from Washington to help nurse him back to health. While there, she came upon a packet of love letters in Lucy's handwriting that confirmed all her suspicions and provided details of the affair. Eleanor was devastated at her husband's betrayal, noting later, "The bottom dropped out of my own particular world . . . " Sober and serious, she knew she had never been able to provide the light-hearted companionship Franklin sometimes sought, but there was an intensity and a depth to their relationship that she needed and valued for her own sense of security and that now seemed to be torn apart.

As she confronted her husband, the two had to decide what to do. Eleanor told him that she would insist on a divorce unless he broke off entirely his affair with Lucy. Sara, too, threatened to cut him off unless he let Lucy go. And Louis Howe underscored the consequences a divorce would have on his promising political career. Franklin agreed he would never see Lucy again.

The affair changed forever the relationship between Eleanor and Franklin. They remained married, but now had to construct a different kind of bond than they had enjoyed in the past. Eleanor spent more time alone, as she thought about what she wanted and needed in her own life. Later she told her closest friends, "I have the memory of an elephant. I can forgive, but I cannot forget."

The other crisis occurred as the result of serious illness. Back in private life, though not particularly interested in either business or legal issues, Roosevelt worked as the vice president responsible for the New York office of the Fidelity and Deposit Company and as a partner in the law firm of Emmet, Marvin & Roosevelt. He involved himself in a variety of civic and charitable causes, as his father had done, and maintained his political connections. In the summer of 1921, he went to Campobello with his family. After sailing, fishing, and taking an unintended dip in the cold waters of the Bay of Fundy, he returned to the house, where he soon felt exhausted and went to bed. In the morning, he found that he was running a fever and discovered that he could not move his legs. To Howe, he said over and over, "I don't know what is the matter with me, Louis. I just don't know." Doctors took a while to make an accurate diagnosis but finally concluded the worst: Roosevelt had polio.

Family members and friends carried him by stretcher to a motorboat, then to a train that took him to a hospital in New York City. There some specialists worried that he might never be able to sit upright again. After months of therapy to see if he could get some movement back and to keep his muscles from wasting away, he returned home just before Christmas, still unable to walk. But he refused to be discouraged and kept up a façade of good cheer.

The next five years were extraordinarily difficult as Roosevelt struggled to regain the use of at least some of his limbs. Mobility in his arms, which had also been affected by the paralyzing disease, came back quickly. His legs only improved a little. Gradually, he learned to move about in a wheelchair, then to walk with crutches, and finally to use heavy leg braces and a cane. He bought a houseboat and spent winters in the warmer Florida Keys. He found that swimming was beneficial, as the buoyancy of water helped support his legs. In the summer of 1924, he heard about a health resort in Warm Springs, Georgia, and he went there to try it out. The warm 89 degree water felt good and seemed to bring about real improvement. He returned the next year, and then, in 1927, bought the complex and made it into a center to treat other polio victims. He continued to visit Warm Springs for the rest of his life, even though he never walked without assistance again.

These years were hard on Eleanor. She called the 1921–1922 period "the most trying winter" of her life. She had been hurt badly by her husband's betrayal, but now he needed her, and she responded to him as fully as she could. When he was tired of doing necessary exercises, she pushed him on like "an old master sergeant" in the words of one doctor. She knew she needed to be strong and able to move around herself, and so she took both swimming and driving lessons. She also learned how to stand up to her mother-in-law for the first time. Sara wanted Franklin, now an invalid, to give up the world of public affairs and return to a quiet life in Hyde Park. Eleanor insisted otherwise.

Eleanor and Louis Howe together were determined to keep Roosevelt's political career alive. Howe still believed FDR could make it to the White House. Polio might make the path more difficult, "but, by gad, legs or no legs, Franklin will be President." Howe understood the vital role Eleanor could play in that effort. It was necessary for her to become more active in the world of politics and, to that end, she joined the Women's Division of the Democratic State Committee. She became editor of its monthly newsletter and learned everything necessary to produce the publication. She also began to travel around the state, helping to set up local political organizations for women.

And she learned what was necessary for public speaking. When she was nervous, her voice became shrill and high-pitched, and she often began to giggle. Howe tutored her and critiqued her performance. "You were terrible," he sometimes told her sternly. "There was nothing funny—why did you laugh? . . . Keep your voice down, and for Heaven's sake, stop that silly giggling." Eleanor listened to the criticism and turned herself from a shy and retiring wife into a forceful personality able to function capably in the outside world.

For his part, Roosevelt kept his spirits up. He believed he could conquer his malady and refused, at least publicly, to feel sorry for himself. Grace Tully, a secretary who worked closely with FDR for years, once remarked that he "never indulged in self-pity or otherwise gave outward indication that he felt annoyance at the restrictions caused by his illness." That may have been a mask, for Roosevelt had long ago learned to hide his true feelings behind an ebullient grin, but it helped him move back into the world of public affairs when he was ready with a greater empathy for the problems of ordinary people than before. Frances Perkins, the social reformer who worked with him for years in Albany and Washington, believed that his illness made him "completely warm-hearted, with humility of spirit and a deeper philosophy." Eleanor, likewise, understood the impact of his effort to deal with polio. "Franklin's illness proved a blessing in disguise," she later wrote, "for it gave him strength and courage he had not had before. He had to think out the fundamentals of living and learn the greatest of all lessons—infinite patience and never-ending persistence."

Roosevelt returned to the tasks he had been doing before his polio attack. He began to work once more at the Fidelity and Deposit Company. He dissolved his law partnership and formed another. And he plunged back into the political world. He helped persuade Al Smith to run for governor of New York again in 1922, and he agreed to be Smith's campaign manager in the quest for the presidency in 1924.

At the 1924 Democratic national convention held in Madison Square Garden in New York, he played an active role. His speech nominating Smith was a high point in what was otherwise a rancorous and divisive gathering. Moving slowly toward the lectern on his braced legs, casting aside his crutches, thrusting his head and shoulders back and smiling broadly as he gripped the lectern, he gave visible proof to the delegates holding their breath as he walked across the stage of his courage in fighting his infirmity. In his speech about Smith, he concluded, "He has a power to strike at error and wrongdoing that makes his adversaries quail before him. He has a personality that carries to every hearer not only the sincerity but the righteousness of what he says. The 'Happy Warrior' of the political battlefield, Alfred E. Smith." The applause that erupted lasted an hour, and the entire event was a tremendous victory for Roosevelt, even though Smith did not get the nomination.

Those who had counted Roosevelt out were wrong. FDR was back.

3

Governor of New York

As Franklin Roosevelt struggled to regain his health in the 1920s, the United States sought to regain its balance after the shock of the Great War. After a rocky start, the economy boomed and prosperity brought with it a period of Republican ascendancy. It was probably to Roosevelt's advantage to be out of what could easily have been a discouraging and unsuccessful scramble for public office. His recovery propelled him onto the national scene at a crucial time.

Americans wanted to put the war behind them. Although the nation had only been an active participant for a year and a half, its involvement had made the crucial difference to the victory. But as the United States Senate rejected the peace treaty signed at Versailles, just outside Paris, and shunned Woodrow Wilson's dream of a League of Nations to settle differences and head off future wars, most Americans were eager to turn away from international involvement and to enjoy the prosperity that beckoned, dedicating themselves to the pursuit of what Warren G. Harding, elected president in 1920, called "normalcy."

The first few difficult years of the postwar decade gave way to a thriving economy. Industrial production nearly doubled, as the index figure of 58 in 1921 increased to 110 in 1929. Per capita income rose from $480 in 1900 to

$681 in 1929, and real earnings—what workers actually had to spend—soared. The automobile industry helped fuel prosperity as it became a huge stimulus for other production, just as the railroad had been in the nineteenth century. After installing the innovative moving assembly line in 1914, Henry Ford's automobile plant in Highland Park, Michigan, assembled a new car every 93 minutes. By 1929, the nation was producing 4,800,000 cars a year, with more than 26 million autos and trucks in use in the United States. "Machinery," Ford declared, "is the new Messiah."

The stock market mirrored the country's exuberant optimism. Though perhaps only one million people, out of a population of well over 100 million, invested in the market, most Americans were aware of the extraordinary increase in the volume and value of stock prices. From 236 million shares traded in 1923, the number rose to 1,125 million in 1928. In that latter year, the price of industrial stocks went up 86.5 points, far higher than the normal rise, in a frenzy of buying activity that continued into the summer of 1929.

Politics reflected the prosperity. The headlong pursuit of wealth led some businessmen to cut corners, and a number of those men had the president's ear. Harding, who looked presidential but found himself overwhelmed by the office, was worried by scandals that began to surface. "I have no trouble with my enemies," he told journalist William Allen White. "But my damned friends, my God-damned friends, White, they're the ones that keep me walking the floor nights!" To Nicholas Murray Butler, president of Columbia University, he confessed, "I knew that this job would be too much for me." Harding died after becoming ill on a trip to the American West before the scandals became public, and he was succeeded by the laconic Calvin Coolidge, who was even more an apostle of the business creed. "The man who builds a factory builds a temple," he once declared. "The man who works there worships there."

Secretary of Commerce Herbert Hoover represented the new prosperity best of all. He was a highly successful mining engineer, who had directed the American relief effort and helped feed starving Europeans during the war. He was a humanitarian who chafed under the doctrinaire conservatism of Harding and Coolidge, and he was sympathetic to some basic progressive goals that sought to rationalize the economy. *American Individualism*, a book he wrote in 1922, underscored a fundamental personal commitment to self-sufficiency. Yet at the same time he recognized the need for government to play a larger role in the economy than before and sought to promote a cooperative relationship between business and government, with business taking the lead. When he ran for president against Al Smith in 1928, he summed up his pervasive optimism that government and business could work together by declaring, "We in America today are nearer to the final triumph over poverty than ever before in the history of any land."

Roosevelt watched the political world carefully. As he regained his strength, he had to decide what to do. He refused an effort to nominate him for the United States Senate in 1926, declaring that he wanted to continue his physical-therapy exercises, noting that "if I devote another two years to them I shall be on my feet again without my braces." At the same time, he acknowledged that he was reluctant to be circumscribed by the Senate and its procedures: "I like administrative or executive work, but do not want to have my hands and feet tied and my wings clipped for six long years." Two years later, hailed by some as a presidential candidate, he declined with the observation, "I am very doubtful whether any Democrat can win in 1928." Instead, he served as Al Smith's campaign manager at the Democratic national convention in

Houston, and helped him become the party's choice. Moving around the convention floor with braces and a cane, leaning on one son's arm, he gave the impression of being healthy and vigorous, well on his way to a recovery from his bout with polio. As in 1924, he was an imposing presence at the lectern. He had become an accomplished orator, and his speech nominating Smith was well-received.

New York Democrats wanted him to run for governor. At first, while continuing therapy at Warm Springs, he refused. Louis Howe thought that Hoover would be president for two terms, and was unsure of FDR's chances in New York in 1928. He also believed that by declining to run, Roosevelt would have the time to learn to walk with just a cane. Marguerite (Missy) LeHand, Roosevelt's secretary, was equally adamant in urging him to say no and stand firm. His daughter Anna, on the other hand, sent a telegram urging him to go ahead, to which he cabled the response, "You ought to be spanked." But Eleanor, aware that only a return to political activity would make her husband happy, agreed with Anna, and eventually Roosevelt told Al Smith that he would accept the nomination if it was offered. In so doing, he may well have understood that he would never be able to walk normally again and made a calculated decision to move on.

Roosevelt threw himself into the campaign and drew on support from all sides. He found himself pitted against Republican nominee Albert Ottinger, a former attorney general. When opponents highlighted FDR's disability and sought to portray him as a weak surrogate for Al Smith, who would continue to control New York, Smith came to his defense with the comment: "A governor does not have to be an acrobat. We do not elect him for his ability to do a double back-flip or a handspring."

Howe was again in charge of the campaign, and others joined the team. Henry Morgenthau, Jr., a Dutchess

County neighbor as interested in agriculture as Roosevelt, went around the state preparing the way for FDR. Raymond Moley, a Barnard College professor of political science, helped provide background on important issues, while James A. Farley, secretary of the Democratic State Committee, who knew and remembered thousands of names and faces, signed on help with political organizing. Samuel I. Rosenman, a young lawyer, provided advice on state problems and drafted speeches, which Roosevelt then rewrote according to his own sense of rhetoric and timing.

Roosevelt spoke out strongly in defense of Al Smith's administration as governor of New York. "Anybody in public life who goes ahead and advocates improvements is called a radical," he declared. "The Democratic Party in this state has gone on and advocated improvements, and it has put them through, and it has been called radical and everything else, and it is keeping on winning, and the Democratic Party in this State will keep on winning as long as it goes ahead with a program of progress." He called for such reforms as an 8-hour day and a 48-hour work week for women and children, an old-age pension scheme, and assistance to the handicapped. Though a two-to-one underdog at the start of the campaign, his efforts made it a close contest by the end.

On election day, Roosevelt won by 25,564 votes out of more than four million cast. In New York state, he ran ahead of Smith, who lost the national election to Hoover by a vote of 21 million to 15 million, as Americans gave notice that they did not want to make changes and risk ending prosperous times. Smith's defeat was a blow to his national ambitions. Roosevelt's victory in New York, on the other hand, indicated that he was a force to be reckoned with in the Democratic Party.

Roosevelt took office as governor determined to control his own administration. Al Smith, having lost his bid to become president, hoped to continue to be a dominant presence in Albany, just as he had been during his eight years as chief executive of New York. When Smith suggested that the new governor keep two of his top associates—Belle Moskowitz as secretary and Robert Moses as secretary of state—Roosevelt listened but did nothing, for he had his own people in mind. "I've *got* to be Governor of the State of New York," he told Frances Perkins, who joined his administration as head of the Labor Department, "and I have got to be it MYSELF."

While FDR was delighted to be in charge of the state, Eleanor was not happy about returning to Albany. "I don't like public life," she said. "I thought when we came back from Washington, we were through with it." Along with Louis Howe, she had helped keep her husband's political career alive, but at the same time she had become a much more independent person. Now she feared that she might have to circumscribe some of her own activities. She did resign from the Democratic State Committee and decided she would no longer speak out on political issues. But she continued to teach three days a week at the Todhunter School in New York City, going down by train on Sunday evening and then returning in midweek to help entertain at the executive mansion. And she remained active in such organizations as the Women's Trade Union League.

On one occasion during the gubernatorial years, a reporter asked her to reflect on the subject "What is a Wife's Job Today?" Eleanor argued that there needed to be mutual respect between husband and wife, and that there had to be "some great common interest" to keep the partnership alive. Though she did not confide in the reporter, Eleanor and Franklin had developed a new kind of alliance in the years following the Lucy Mercer affair. Physical intimacy was gone, and at Hyde Park Eleanor even built her own house—Val-Kill—on the property, which she shared with her closest female friends. Each partner in the marriage enjoyed the company of others, and yet, despite what both perceived as a necessary distance, they needed one another and they worked together regularly, perhaps hoping for something more than either was able to give. Each still had the capacity to hurt the other and did so from time to time, then tried to make amends. Once, as FDR was sailing to France to pick up his mother, who had come down with pneumonia, Eleanor wrote to him apologizing for her testiness. "We are really very dependent on each other though we do see so little of each other," she noted. And then she concluded, "Dear love to you. I miss you and hate to feel you so far away."

Assuming office as governor, FDR considered himself part of the progressive tradition, so important in early twentieth-century America. He wanted state agencies to be stronger to provide necessary oversight; he wanted professional administrative appointments to take precedence over patronage to root out the corruption that frequently accompanied state spending; he wanted greater support for state social-service activities to assist those who lacked resources of their own; and, following the example of those who railed against the largest industrial trusts, he wanted greater regulation of business practices.

Though he faced a Republican legislature, he was able to push through an executive budget, mandated by a state constitutional amendment in 1927, that gave him some flexibility in initiating other programs. Roosevelt was concerned about farmers, who were steadily losing ground nationwide as overproduction drove prices down. To assist them, he moved to reduce the amount of money rural counties had to contribute to the costs of constructing state highways, to commit the state to help with rural education costs, and to implement a cooperative-dairy-marketing organization. Seeking cheaper power for everyone, he sought to develop public water-power resources, particularly in the vicinity of the St. Lawrence River, and, at the same time, to establish workable regulation of private utility companies that often gouged their customers. He came to the defense of the labor movement. He pushed to end injunctions without a hearing in labor disputes, continued to demand an 8-hour day for public workers and a 48-hour week for women and children, and called for better workmen's compensation laws. And he supported the need for old-age pensions funded by "contributions from public resources, employers, and the workers themselves."

But Roosevelt really made his mark by his aggressive effort to do something about the ravages of the Great Depression. In his first year in office, the United States suffered a catastrophic economic collapse. Despite a rising standard of living, a number of serious problems had been largely ignored. Wealth was concentrated in the hands of the few, as profits rose more rapidly than wages and, while many farmers and workers could afford an automobile and other modern appliances, they did not have the purchasing power to keep the economy running smoothly. The Federal Reserve system had been created in 1914 to provide some financial oversight, but banks were overly active in promoting the wave of speculation and the larger structure lacked mechanisms to respond in the event of a collapse. There were troubling indicators in 1929, as residential building began to drop off, and the rate of growth in the automobile industry began to decline. But those trends went unnoticed until the stock market bubble burst in the fall of that year.

The speculative frenzy could not last forever. The basically unregulated stock market had lost all connection with the realities of industrial production; it was something like a child's soap bubble that grew ever bigger until its inevitable pop. In September 1929, the stock market faltered, rallied, then fell again. Refusing to worry, Professor Irving Fisher of Yale University declared, "Stock prices have reached what looks like a permanently high plateau." At the end of October, prices dropped even more dramatically, and Tuesday, October 29—Black Tuesday—was the worst day the market had ever known. That collapse was bad enough, but the crash continued. It need not have caused a massive depression, if the economy itself had been stronger, but weaknesses grew worse as the collapse eroded the purchasing power and shattered the confidence of the businessmen who might have kept the economy afloat.

Massive unemployment was the result. The number stood under 500,000 in October 1929, but reached more than four million in January 1930. It hit eight million in early 1931 and twelve million in 1932. At least one-quarter of all employable Americans could not find jobs, and many more were underemployed. Workers and farmers alike were devastated by the Great Depression, and large states like New York were particularly hard-hit. In 1932, there were a million unemployed people in New York City alone. Many defaulted on mortgages and had to move into progressively smaller apartments. Bread lines, providing at least simple sustenance, stretched around the block in city after city. And that same year, both Bing Crosby and Rudy Vallee recorded the song that echoed the despair: "Brother, Can You Spare a Dime?"

Roosevelt's record-setting plurality of 725,000 votes in his 1930 reelection victory over Republican opponent Charles H. Tuttle made him willing to move ahead. As the economic crisis got worse, he wrote, "There is no question in my mind that it is time for the country to become fairly radical for a generation. History shows that where this occurs occasionally, nations are saved from revolution."

Something had to be done about unemployment. To that end, Roosevelt asked for studies from the Joint

Committee on Unemployment Relief of the State Board of Welfare and the New York State Charities Aid Association. With the magnitude of the crisis clear, he called the legislature into special session in August 1931. Concluding that assistance "must be extended by government not as a matter of charity, but as a matter of social duty," he sought passage of a $20 million appropriation financed by an increase in the income tax. New York's State Unemployment Relief Act, passed the next month, was the first such law in any state to help the jobless. It created the Temporary Emergency Relief Administration (TERA), headed by Harry Hopkins, an eager and energetic social worker, who quickly got to work. In the next year and a half, the new agency handled 412,882 relief cases and spent nearly $137 million in state funds.

All the while, Roosevelt had his eye on the presidency. After his sweeping reelection victory, others, too, recognized that he was a prime candidate. Will Rogers, the well-known comedian and down-to-earth political commentator, observed of the New York election in November 1930, "The Democrats nominated their president yesterday, Franklin D. Roosevelt."

Looking for help in generating ideas to deal with the economic crisis, Roosevelt gathered around him a group of university professors. At the suggestion of speechwriter Samuel Rosenman, the shrewd and articulate Raymond Moley, who had worked with FDR on his 1928 campaign for governor, helped recruit others to bolster the team. Rexford G. Tugwell, an audacious Columbia University economist and expert on agriculture, and Adolf A. Berle, Jr., a brilliant and precocious faculty member at the Columbia Law School who was interested in corporate influence, agreed to join the group. Together they became what FDR called his "privy council," which received a new name when a *New York Times* journalist referred to the group as the "brains trust," later shortened to simply "brain trust."

Those advisers bandied about a variety of ideas. Bigness, they believed, was a fact of life, and business needed to be regulated, not broken apart. They concluded that under-consumption lay behind the deadly depression, for business had not passed on gains from increased productivity to workers who could then use their purchasing power to keep the economy growing, and so they looked for ways to revive consumption. At the same time, they struggled to find a way of creating greater stability in agriculture, where overproduction was driving prices down to such a degree that small farmers, in particular, could not survive.

Roosevelt began to speak out about national problems. At the annual meeting of the nation's governors, held in French Lick, Indiana, in mid-1931, he outlined a program for dealing with the economic crisis that included reducing tariffs and taxes, creating a more progressive tax system, and providing both unemployment and health insurance. In the spring of 1932, with ideas generated by the "brain trust," he gave a nationwide radio address that called for comprehensive planning to restore purchasing power, public-works projects to help the unemployed, and mortgage relief to aid small homeowners. Above all, he asserted the need to remember "the forgotten man at the bottom of the economic pyramid" who needed the government's help.

Radio, for Roosevelt, became an increasingly important tool, which could help mobilize the support of ordinary Americans. "It seems to me," he had noted a few years before, "that radio is gradually bringing to the ears of our people matters of interest concerning their country which they refused to consider in the daily press with their eyes." FDR understood that radio could help him circumvent the opposition of press barons who opposed him and could help create a new kind of connection between leaders and citizens of the United States.

Over and over, FDR stressed the need of "imaginative and purposeful planning." And he insisted in May 1932, in an address at Oglethorpe University in Georgia, that aggressive action was necessary, proclaiming confidently: "The country needs, and unless I mistake its temper, the country demands bold, persistent experimentation. It is common sense to take a method and try it: If it fails, admit it frankly and try another. But above all, try something."

By the time of the Democratic national convention, held in Chicago in 1932, Roosevelt was the frontrunner, but his nomination was not assured. Al Smith, following his overwhelming defeat in 1928, had renounced further presidential ambitions, then changed his mind, announced his availability, and gathered a small following. It was not large enough to gain him the nomination, but could be used to stop Roosevelt, from whom he had become increasingly estranged as a result of FDR's insistence on keeping his gubernatorial authority in his own hands. In the first ballot for president, Roosevelt had $666\frac{1}{4}$ votes to $201\frac{3}{4}$ for Smith and $90\frac{1}{4}$ for John Nance Garner of Texas. But the convention was still bound by a rule mandating a two-thirds majority and, unless Roosevelt got over the top quickly, his support could erode in favor of a compromise candidate. Two more ballots brought only small gains. Later that same day, as delegates returned from a recess, California abandoned Garner and gave its 44 votes to Roosevelt, and other states quickly followed suit. FDR was the Democratic nominee.

Roosevelt then took a dramatic step and flew to Chicago to make his acceptance speech in person. Such an action was unprecedented and symbolically important in the midst of hard times. It also demonstrated clearly that FDR was physically ready to take on a grueling campaign.

Standing before the convention, he declared confidently, "I have started out on the tasks that lie ahead by breaking the absurd traditions that the candidate should remain in professed ignorance of what has happened for weeks until he is formally notified of that event many weeks later. . . . You have nominated me and I know it, and I am here to thank you for the honor." He concluded, "I pledge you, I pledge myself, to a new deal for the American people." That phrase, which had an electrifying effect on the convention, became the slogan for Roosevelt's campaign.

The Republicans were in trouble in 1932. Hoover, who had come to the presidency on a wave of optimism, had been discredited by his handling of the Great Depression. His hopes for reform vanished in the turbulence of the economic catastrophe. He refused to accept the callous advice of Andrew Mellon, his wealthy secretary of the treasury, who urged him to "liquidate labor, liquidate stocks, liquidate the farmers, liquidate real estate," but he had no effective alternative. Constrained by his own commitment to individualism, he was unable to push the government to take the kind of aggressive action that might have helped. The task of aiding the unemployed, he believed, belonged to either local government or private charity. Federal relief would both unbalance the budget and erode the character of those individuals accepting help.

Hoover understood that the Depression was a worldwide phenomenon. He knew how closely the American economy was connected to that of Europe in the complicated aftermath of World War I, as American loans helped vanquished nations make reparations payments to the victors. But his blame of outside forces for causing the Depression circumscribed his response to the catastrophe at home.

Hoover tried unsuccessfully to provide encouragement to his constituents. He chose to avoid using the term "panic," which he felt had a frightening connotation, and picked the term "depression" instead, only to see it take on even worse association. He tried to look on the bright side of the calamity with the claim that no one had starved, but could not refute education officials who claimed that there were about 20,000 malnourished children in the New York City schools alone in 1932. He encouraged members of his administration to make optimistic forecasts about the future, and he did so himself, but those had no connection to reality, leading the Republican national chairman to note, "Every time an Administration official gives out an optimistic statement about business conditions, the market immediately drops."

Hoover took a number of important steps but they did not go far enough. He increased spending on federal public works projects and tried to persuade state and local officials to do the same, then undermined the possibility of large-scale spending by an effort to balance the budget by raising taxes. The need for a balanced budget was an article of faith for both economists and ordinary Americans, an implicit pledge that the nation would preserve the value of its currency and, by so doing, encourage new investment.

Hoover appointed a number of committees to investigate problems and propose solutions, but gave them no authority to take aggressive action. The President's Emergency Committee for Employment (PECE), established in the fall of 1930, sought to promote voluntary municipal efforts to help those without jobs, then gave way in six months to the President's Organization on Unemployment Relief (POUR). Its head, Walter S. Gifford, president of American Telephone and Telegraph, had to confess to a congressional committee that he did not have an accurate figure for the number of unemployed, nor did he know how to deal with the catastrophe. Neither PECE nor POUR made any significant progress in dealing with the unprecedented crisis.

Hoover also resisted a number of congressional efforts to gather unemployment statistics, create a federal unemployment service, and provide funding for public works. His effort at optimism led him to claim, despite evidence to the contrary, that because of "an aroused sense of public responsibility, those in destitution and their children are actually receiving more regular and more adequate care than even in normal times."

Only reluctantly did he agree to the creation of the Reconstruction Finance Corporation (RFC) in early 1932. Patterned after the War Finance Corporation that had helped fund the building of manufacturing plants after the nation's entrance into the Great War, the RFC made emergency loans to banks, railroads, building-and-loan societies, and other organizations. It helped, to be sure, but still was too little, too late.

The situation was becoming increasingly desperate as each year the Great Depression worsened. Voluntary measures were simply inadequate, as charitable organizations exhausted their resources and municipal and state governments lacked the means to make much of a difference. "We can no longer depend on passing the hat, and rattling the tin cup," Kansas journalist William Allen White wrote. "We have gone to the bottom of the barrel."

Hoover found himself the focus of blame. Shanty towns in most major cities came to be called "Hoovervilles." Newspapers spread over a person's body to keep warm became "Hoover blankets." An empty pants pocket pulled inside out became a "Hoover flag." Jokes, which sometimes provide insight into popular mood, were now at Hoover's expense. In one, the president asked for a nickel to call a friend. An aide gave him a dime with the comment, "Here, call them both."

Hoover himself grew more and more gloomy. "It was like sitting in a bath of ink to sit in his room," Secretary of State Henry L. Stimson remarked. Hoover had made his mark as an administrator, not a politician, and had not run for public office until he sought the presidency in 1928. Though he was highly skilled at running bureaucratic organizations, he lacked the political skills to cajole various competing interests to compromise and come to a necessary consensus. He was thin-skinned and once confessed, "I do not believe that I have the mental attitude or the politician's manner . . . and above all I am too sensitive to political mud." Now he found the barrage of criticism hard to take. Byron Price, a journalist who saw him occasionally, observed in 1932, "He didn't look to me like the Hoover I had been seeing. His hair was rumpled. He was almost crouching behind his desk, and he burst out at me with a volley of angry words—not against me or the press, but against the politicians and the foreign governments—with absolutely unbridled language and never hesitating to mention a name. . . . I've never heard anybody do a better or more vituperative job of laying out some of his political enemies than Mr. Hoover did, in language he must have learned in a mining camp."

His response to the Bonus Army made a difficult situation worse. American veterans of the Great War had been promised a bonus, payable in 1945, in the Adjusted Compensation Act of 1924. Now 15,000 to 20,000 of them came to Washington in the spring of 1932 to lobby Congress to pay the bonus immediately. Unemployed and destitute, most of them simply could not wait for another decade and a half. After the House of Representatives passed such a measure but the Senate balked, about half of the Bonus Expeditionary Force—named after the Allied Expeditionary Force that fought the war—remained in the nation's capital. Most members of this motley group stayed across the Anacostia River, in the southeast sector of the city, in ramshackle shelters made of packing crates and other debris; some occupied empty buildings in the downtown area along Pennsylvania Avenue near the National Gallery and the Federal Trade Commission. The president never went out to greet them. "HOOVER LOCKS SELF IN WHITE HOUSE," a headline in the *New York Daily News* proclaimed. The men were orderly, even as the summer turned hot and humid. Will Rogers commented that former soldiers held "the record for being the best behaved" of any "hungry men assembled anywhere in the world." But on July 28, the government decided to move them out. In a scuffle with police on Pennsylvania Avenue, two veterans were killed. As reinforcements moved in from the Anacostia area, federal troops, led by Army Chief of Staff Douglas MacArthur, with assistance from younger officers Dwight D. Eisenhower and George Patton, brought in tanks and burned the camp down. MacArthur claimed that he was fighting "a mob . . . animated by the essence of revolution," while the White House declared that the men who had fought back were "entirely of the Communist element." Most Americans, viewing the president with contempt, disagreed. At the governor's mansion in Albany, Eleanor Roosevelt read about the confrontation with "a feeling of horror," while FDR was furious at the president, declaring, "There is nothing inside the man but jelly." Hoover, seeking reelection in a futile effort at self-vindication, never had a chance.

Yet Roosevelt initially generated little enthusiasm with the public at large. He had to fight to overcome the impression that he was a political lightweight. Critics charged that he lacked strong convictions and was not capable of making difficult decisions. They claimed, with some truth, that in his quest for the presidency he sought to straddle issues, without taking a firm stand, as had been the case in his effort to appeal to both supporters and opponents of Prohibition. When, on another occasion, after long claiming he was an internationalist who had served in Woodrow Wilson's administration for eight years, he had withdrawn his support for American entrance into the World Court, in a bald effort to gain isolationist support, Eleanor had been so angry that she refused to speak to him for several days. Roosevelt was, columnist Walter Lippmann observed, the master of the "balanced antithesis."

As he threw himself into the campaign, he did show occasional inconsistency in his views. He criticized Hoover for being "committed to the idea that we ought to center control of everything in Washington as rapidly as possible," while demanding bold federal action to deal with the economic crisis. He condemned Republican efforts to maintain a high tariff, making it more costly for consumers to buy goods from abroad and making American goods more expensive in the absence of external competition, but shifted course so many times that his position ended up little different than Hoover's. In a speech about agricultural issues in Topeka, Kansas, there was minimal substance, for, as Raymond Moley observed, FDR wanted to win Midwestern support "without waking up the dogs of the East." And, even as he stood by his record in New York of assisting the unemployed, and conveyed the impression that he would do the same thing at the national level, he condemned Hoover for heading "the greatest spending Administration in peace times in all our history," and promised that he would cut federal spending by 25 percent.

After sometimes calling for a New Freedom approach of breaking apart large industrial combinations, and other times favoring a New Nationalism effort to regulate big business, Roosevelt tried to synthesize his views. In a speech at the Commonwealth Club in San Francisco in

September 1932, he declared, "Our industrial plant is built; the problem just now is whether under existing conditions it is not overbuilt." A reappraisal of national values was necessary: "Our task now is not discovery or exploitation of natural resources, or necessarily producing more goods. It is the soberer, less dramatic business of administering resources and plants already in hand, of seeking to reestablish foreign markets for our surplus production, of meeting the problem of underconsumption, of adjusting production to consumption, of distributing wealth and products more equitably, of adapting existing economic organization to the service of the people."

Roosevelt's campaign speeches, taken together, did foreshadow many of the initiatives that followed. But they lacked specificity, for FDR knew that Hoover was in serious political trouble and, understandably, did not want to squander his advantage by needlessly alienating various constituent groups.

On balance, most Americans had little sense of what Roosevelt would do as president. He remained, in Walter Lippmann's words, "a kind of amiable boy scout" rather than a leader who would take charge. On another occasion, Lippmann was even more critical when he wrote, "Franklin Roosevelt is no tribune of the people. He is no enemy of entrenched privilege. He is a pleasant man who, without any important qualifications for the office, would very much like to be president."

Despite such concerns, on election day Roosevelt swept into office. He received 22.8 million votes to 15.75 million for Hoover, and won by a margin of 472–59 in the Electoral College. He carried the South and West, though he lost parts of the East, but he still managed to hold on to the support of the urban immigrants who had voted for Al Smith four years before. While the election was an overwhelming victory for FDR, it was at the same time a repudiation of Hoover. After years of battling the Great Depression, people were willing to try anyone else.

Roosevelt had Democratic majorities in both houses of Congress. He had the good will of the American people behind him. Now he had to decide how to deal with the problems of a nation in serious distress.

4

The First Hundred Days

Franklin Roosevelt was president-elect, but still had to wait four months until taking office. And in that interval between his election in November 1932 and his inauguration in March 1933, conditions deteriorated further. National income was now half of what it had been before the Depression, as the economy ground to a halt. The long, cold winter took its toll, as the number of unemployed Americans reached the 13 million mark. Nor was there an end in sight. The stock market crash had wiped out the assets of many large investors, hampering their ability to keep businesses providing goods and services at full tilt. Bank failures across the country now swept away the savings of millions of small investors, leaving them with no resources at all. In his diary, adviser Rexford Tugwell noted "a profound sense of uneasiness" that winter. "Never, in modern times, I should think, has there been so widespread unemployment and such moving distress from sheer hunger and cold." Roosevelt had won the election, but now the overriding question was: What would he do?

Hoover knew what he wanted from his successor. Discouraged by his loss and concerned about the course the new Democratic administration might take, he sought to get Roosevelt to do nothing less than endorse policies the outgoing administration had tried to put into place. In early November, just after the election, he took an unprecedented step and sent FDR a long telegram noting the need to deal with the question of international debt and asking for "an opportunity to confer with you personally at some convenient date in the near future."

Hoover continued to believe, with some insight, that the Great Depression was a contagion from abroad, rooted in the economic chaos created by the Great War. The United States had lent considerable sums of money to other nations during the struggle and now wanted those debts repaid, but the worldwide economic crisis made repayment difficult. Hoover had persuaded a reluctant Congress to grant a moratorium the year before, but there was a general unwillingness to extend the moratorium, and so Hoover sought Roosevelt's help.

Roosevelt had a different view of the Great Depression. He believed it resulted from internal structural weaknesses in the capitalist system, and argued it was necessary to implement necessary reforms before dealing with the outside world. As Raymond Moley, a member of the "brain trust," observed, Roosevelt and his advisers "were agreed that the heart of the recovery program was and must be domestic."

An awkward first meeting took place in the White House toward the end of November, then a second one in January. Roosevelt listened to Hoover's explanations politely without making any commitments of his own. Hoover was furious at Roosevelt's unwillingness to help and regarded the president-elect as "amiable, pleasant, anxious to be of service, very badly informed and of comparatively little vision." He made one final attempt in mid-February, with a long letter to FDR, pointing to public doubts about Roosevelt's commitment to a balanced budget and fears about the possibility of a dictatorship. "I am convinced," he wrote, "that a very early statement by you upon two or three policies of your Administration would serve greatly to restore confidence and cause a resumption of the march of recovery." Hoover knew exactly what he was doing. As he noted in a letter to Republican Senator David Reed of Pennsylvania, "I realize that if these declarations be made by the President-elect, he will have ratified the whole major program of the Republican Administration; that is, it means the abandonment of 90% of the so-called new deal."

Roosevelt had no intention of associating himself with Hoover's failed policies. But his intentions remained vague, even to his closest advisers. Above all, he believed he needed to maintain independence of action until he had the authority to deal appropriately with what sometimes appeared to be insurmountable problems. After that, the course remained unclear. The "brain trust" continued to generate ideas for programs on all fronts, though as Moley later noted, reflecting on the various initiatives that emerged, "to look at these policies as the result of a unified plan was to believe that the accumulation of stuffed snakes, baseball pictures, school flags, old tennis shoes, carpenter's tools, geometry books, and chemistry sets in a boy's bedroom could have been put there by an interior decorator."

Roosevelt spent considerable time putting his cabinet together. He wanted notable figures, but not so impressive that they would outshine him. The cabinet started out as an able, if not an exciting, group that included a number of prominent names. For secretary of state, he chose Cordell Hull, a courtly southerner who had spent a long and distinguished career in Congress. Fiscal policy was Hull's passion, and he was dedicated to the notion of lower tariffs and freer trade to promote international peace and prosperity. For secretary of the treasury, FDR wanted Carter Glass, a Democratic senator from Virginia who was an expert on public finance, but he was ailing and was also fearful that the new administration would embark on a policy of inflation, which he opposed. When he declined the position, Roosevelt settled on William Woodin, a railroad industrialist, lifelong Republican, and personal friend. For the secretary of agriculture, he chose Henry A. Wallace, editor of a farm paper in Iowa, who had been a progressive Republican until he had broken with the party in 1928 over issues of farm relief and high tariffs. For secretary of the interior, FDR picked Harold Ickes, a crusty old progressive and self-styled curmudgeon, cautious, careful, and scrupulously honest. For attorney general, he selected Homer Cummings, a longtime Democrat who had served as Roosevelt's floor manager at the Democratic convention. And for secretary of labor, he chose Frances Perkins, with whom he had worked in New York, to be the first woman member of any cabinet. Women's rights leaders—and sympathetic men—were delighted with the long-overdue appointment of a woman and with the choice of Perkins. The news, Harvard University law professor Felix Frankfurter wrote, "exhilarates me." James Farley, another New York ally, became postmaster general, in which position he could use his astute political skills in making useful patronage appointments.

Other people had a major role working with FDR. The "brain trust" that featured Moley, Tugwell, and Berle continued to provide advice and to suggest policy alternatives. Louis Howe was still in the picture as a political advisor, though perhaps less influential than before, as was Samuel Rosenman, who became one of Roosevelt's favorite speechwriters. Harry Hopkins, likewise part of the New York team that moved to Washington, handled relief efforts and, in time, virtually any other task to which he was assigned as he became the president's right-hand man.

And then there was Eleanor. She was ambivalent about this next step in her husband's career and its implications for her own life. "You're always pleased to have any one you're very devoted to have what he wants," she said after the election. Then she added, "It's an extremely serious thing to undertake, you know. . . . It is not something you just . . . say you're pleased about." She was determined to play her part, as always, in her own way. "There isn't going to be any First Lady," she told her students at the Todhunter School. 'There is just going to be plain, ordinary Mrs. Roosevelt. And that's all." But she understood there was more at stake, as she told her increasingly close companion Lorena Hickok: "I never wanted to be a President's wife. Now I shall have to work out my own salvation. I'm afraid it may be a little difficult."

During the long interregnum, Roosevelt was fortunate to survive an assassination attempt. In Miami in mid-February, after an 11-day cruise, he traveled in an open car to Bay Front Park to speak briefly in the evening to a crowd of thousands of people eager to see the president-elect. Vincent Astor, owner of the yacht on which he had been sailing and his companion in the car, was concerned about the closeness of the crowd and remarked twice that it would be easy for a crank to shoot at them. Roosevelt shrugged off the warning, as he had an earlier note of caution from John Nance Garner, his incoming vice president; then he quoted his cousin Theodore as saying, "The only real danger from an assassin is from one who does not care whether he loses his own life in the act or not. Most of the crazy ones can be spotted first." As he finished his remarks to the crowd, Mayor Anton J. Cermak of Chicago approached the car and spoke to him. As he was moving away, Joseph Zangara, a short, curly-headed man, jumped up and, from a distance of about 35 feet, fired a pistol at Roosevelt. The president-elect was not hit by any of the five shots, but an unlucky Cermak fell to the ground. Roosevelt insisted that the Secret Service agents stop the car, and pick up Cermak to take him to the hospital. Cradling him in his arms, he repeated over and over, "Tony, keep quiet—don't move. It won't hurt you if you keep quiet." Cermak made it to the hospital, only to die a few weeks later. Roosevelt had not simply survived but had remained remarkably cool in the face of potentially catastrophic danger.

As if problems of personal safety were not enough, Roosevelt had to face an impending banking crisis. Banks had been failing for the past few years as frightened investors, afraid the financial institutions would collapse, withdrew their funds, thereby precipitating the very breakdown they hoped to avoid. Problems began in the West and, in October 1932, the governor of Nevada proclaimed a bank holiday, shutting down the system to prevent it from completely falling apart. Even so, failures in other western states continued, creating growing concern. In mid-February 1933, the governor of Michigan followed in the footsteps of his Nevada counterpart, declaring a similar holiday to forestall a collapse. A week-and-a-half later, a run on banks in Baltimore led the governor of Maryland to announce a banking holiday in his state. As people stood in long lines with paper bags and satchels to withdraw whatever money they could, banks all over the country teetered on the brink of disaster. Agnes Meyer, wife of one of the federal reserve governors, noted in her diary that Hoover was leaving office "to the sound of crashing banks" and observed, "World literally rocking beneath our feet." By the time of the inauguration on March 4, 38 states had closed their banks, with most of the others not far behind. In a rare move, the New York Stock Exchange shut down, as did the Chicago Board of Trade.

Outwardly, Roosevelt seemed serenely confident in his ability to deal with the crisis. He knew that people everywhere were looking to him to take action and lift the cloud of gloom around the country. On inauguration day, he attended a brief church service, where Endicott Peabody, his old headmaster at Groton, prayed to God to "bless Thy servant, Franklin." On his way to the Capitol to take the oath of office and deliver his inaugural address, he stopped at the Mayflower Hotel to speak with advisors about how to deal with the banking problem.

The inaugural address, delivered after Roosevelt repeated the oath of office, was a vivid contrast to the dismal pronouncements Hoover had been making for the past three years. Roosevelt was reassuring: "I am certain that my fellow Americans expect that on my induction into the Presidency I will address them with a candor and a decision which the present situation of our Nation impels. This is preeminently the time to speak the truth, the whole truth, frankly and boldly. Nor need we shrink from honestly facing conditions in our country today. This great Nation will endure as it has endured, will revive and will prosper." And then he spoke the lines, pausing at the appropriate point, that people remembered for years to come: "So, first of all, let me assert my firm belief that the only thing we have to fear is fear itself—nameless, unreasoning, unjustified terror which paralyzes needed efforts to convert retreat into advance."

With biblical imagery, he lashed out at the nation's bankers. "Our distress comes from no failure of substance," he declared. "We are stricken by no plague of locusts. . . . Plenty is at our doorstep, but a generous use of it languishes in the very sight of the supply. Primarily this is because rulers of the exchange of mankind's goods have failed through their own stubbornness and their own incompetence, have admitted their failure, and have abdicated. . . . The money changers have fled from their high seats in the temple of our civilization. We may now restore that temple to the ancient truths."

FDR proclaimed his intention of taking whatever steps were necessary to deal with the depression. "This nation asks for action, and action now," he declared. He was prepared to work collaboratively with Congress, but if legislators failed to act, "I shall not evade the clear course of duty that will then confront me. I shall ask the Congress for the one remaining instrument to meet the crisis—broad Executive power to wage a war against the emergency, as great as the power that would be given to me if we were in fact invaded by a foreign foe."

With that one step, Roosevelt restored a sense of hope throughout the country. No longer was he evasive, reluctant to speak out. No longer did he stumble his way through a speech, as he had in his first campaign. With ringing tones and a resonant voice, he made it clear that he was prepared to act, and people, desperate to believe that conditions could indeed improve, were eager to follow. "America hasn't been as happy in three years as they are today," comic Will Rogers said. "The whole country is with him. Even if what he does is wrong they are with him. Just so he does something. If he burned down the Capitol we would cheer and say, 'Well, he at least got a fire started, anyhow.'" In the course of the next week, nearly 500,000 Americans wrote to FDR in a pattern that continued for the duration of his presidency.

The most pressing problem demanding immediate action was the banking crisis. The day after the inauguration, the new president issued two proclamations, one calling Congress into special session a few days hence, the other declaring a four-day national banking holiday, and, at the same time, he suspended trading in gold, to prevent the loss of gold reserves as confidence in banks eroded and to provide flexibility to deal with currency issues. The new secretary of the treasury collaborated with his predecessor, who stayed around to help hammer out a bill that could be presented to Congress when it reconvened. It was a frantic and frenetic time. As Moley later recalled, "Confusion, haste, the dread of making mistakes, the consciousness of responsibility for the economic well-being of millions of people, made mortal inroads on the health of some of us . . . and left the rest of us ready to snap at our own images in the mirror."

When the special session of the solidly Democratic Congress convened at about 1:00 P.M. on March 9, the speaker of the house read the banking bill aloud, for printed copies were not yet available. The House passed it unanimously, after but 38 minutes of debate. The Senate took a little longer, but still approved it early in the evening by a vote of 73–7. At 8:36 P.M., Roosevelt signed the Emergency Banking Act into law. It was a conservative measure that approved actions the president had already taken, gave the Federal Reserve Board the power to issue new bank notes, authorized the reopening of banks that had adequate assets, and arranged for the reorganization of those that did not.

On Sunday evening, March 12, at 10:00 P.M. in Washington, FDR spoke to the nation on the radio in the first of what came to be called his fireside chats. An estimated 60 million Americans tuned in to listen to the president. In soothing tones, in the same deep and resonant voice people had heard in the inaugural address, he told them about the new law and said, "I can assure you that it is safer to keep your money in a reopened bank than under the mattress." And he closed by asking for their cooperation. "We have provided the machinery to restore our financial system; it is up to you to support and make it work," he declared. "It is your problem no less than it is mine. Together we cannot fail."

People responded overwhelmingly to a masterful performance. Letters pouring into the White House reflected the extraordinary connection FDR had established with his listeners. That very night, Mildred I. Goldstein of Joliet, Illinois, wrote, "You are the first President to come into our homes; to make us feel you are working for us; to let us know what you are doing." Two days later, James A. Green of Cincinnati, Ohio, sent a letter saying, "It almost seemed the other night, sitting in my easy chair in the library, that you were across the room from me."

After the banking bill came an effort to cut the budget. The conventional wisdom was that a balanced budget was necessary to maintain confidence and thereby promote investment, which would, in turn, help the economy to revive. To that end, FDR requested authority to slash approximately $500 million in payments to veterans and federal employees. "Too often in recent history," he declared, "liberal governments have been wrecked on rocks of loose fiscal policy." Though some legislative members still remembered grimly the sad story of the Bonus Army, that bill, too, passed and on March 20, the Economy Act became law.

Then came a measure to end the failed Prohibition experiment that had sought to circumscribe the sale of alcohol. The lame-duck Congress the month before had endorsed what was to become the Twenty-First Amendment to the Constitution, repealing the Eighteenth Amendment, but it still had to be ratified by the states before it took effect. Roosevelt now asked for a measure amending the act that had implemented Prohibition and legalizing beer with the relatively weak 3.2 percent alcoholic content. On March 22, he got what he wanted and signed the bill. Legal at long last, the beer, however weak, boosted people's spirits and brought in tax revenue.

Roosevelt was on a roll. Initially, he had anticipated that the special session of Congress would adjourn after dealing with the banking crisis, but now he sensed the opportunity to move ahead with proposals to deal with various promises that were part of the program he had come to call the New Deal.

FDR knew he had to address the needs of the unemployed. On March 14, he brought up the idea of a conservation corps with his cabinet. Long concerned about conservation issues, he saw the possibility of combining environmental activism with economic relief through the provision of government-funded jobs. The next day, officials charged with developing that scheme came back with a plan for a tree-planting initiative, as well as a proposal for public works and another for grants to the states to be used for relief. On March 21, Roosevelt sent another message to Congress asking for all of those initiatives. Congress acted quickly and, within a matter of weeks, the president signed several of the initiatives into law.

The Civilian Conservation Corps (CCC) authorized hiring about 250,000 young, unmarried men to work on forestry projects aimed at beautifying the nation. It paid them a living wage of a dollar a day, which helped provide a measure of relief. In return, they built bridges, trails, and firebreaks in the woods, worked on flood-control projects, and sought to clean up and improve the nation's national parks. The idea, according to Moley, was to create an initiative to provide what philosopher William James had once called the "moral equivalent of war." The program was enormously popular throughout the 1930s.

Close behind came creation of the Federal Emergency Relief Administration (FERA), patterned after a similar agency established in New York State during FDR's term as governor. Roosevelt understood there might be political advantages to providing relief at the national level. He had long tangled with Tammany Hall in New York, which drew its support from the immigrants and other members of the working class for whom it provided welfare services. To Tugwell, FDR mused "that just possibly Tammany could be undercut by taking from it the responsibility for the unemployed. . . . Tammany might be ruined if relief was really organized. People on relief would have no use for Tammany's services. They'd be independent." Even more important was the need to help those who could find no work. To head the new FERA, Roosevelt chose Harry Hopkins, who had led the New York relief organization, and he quickly began to spend the money allocated to provide direct assistance to the states, which would in turn support those most in need. The creation of FERA jobs provided a huge boost to the morale of the unemployed and helped many get through hard times.

Agriculture was another high priority. After prospering during the Great War, with a call for increased production that was quickly absorbed by soldiers and civilians in need around the world, farmers found themselves hurting throughout the 1920s, as markets dried up and overproduction drove prices down. The first congressional proposals to address the problem were vetoed by Calvin Coolidge. A Federal Farm Board created during the Hoover administration tried to purchase surplus crops to sell later when prices improved, but the failure to cut production doomed the effort, and agricultural income dropped by nearly 60 percent during the Depression. Even though crops were growing in the fields, farmers could not harvest and sell them profitably and, in 1933, about 20,000 farmers a month were losing their land to bank foreclosures.

Roosevelt had been deliberately vague about agriculture during the campaign. With many different kinds of farmers eager to make their voices heard, he had insisted that farm leaders agree on the kind of bill they wanted. Secretary of Agriculture Henry Wallace, drawing on the expertise of economists around the country, mobilized support for what was called the "domestic allotment" plan. It sought to restrict acreage and to pay farmers who agreed to cut back on production with money raised from a tax levied on processing at every stage of the agricultural cycle. The hope was to provide farmers with the same purchasing power they had enjoyed before the war.

FDR acknowledged his own questions about what approach was best as he sent a bill incorporating Wallace's plan to Congress on March 16. "I tell you frankly that it is a new and untrod path," he declared, "but I tell you with equal frankness that an unprecedented condition calls for the trial of new means to rescue agriculture." To reporters, he noted that any farm bill "is in the nature of an experiment. We all recognize that. My position toward farm legislation is that we ought to do something to increase the value of farm products and if the darn thing doesn't work, we can say so quite frankly, but at least try it."

The House of Representatives quickly passed the measure; the Senate at first balked. As Tugwell observed, "For real radicals . . . it is not enough; for conservatives it is too much; for Jefferson Democrats it is a new control which they distrust. For the economic philosophy which it represents there are no defenders at all."

In the Senate, there was powerful pressure to make sure the bill would promote inflation. Making the same argument the Populists—agrarian activists—had made in the late nineteenth century, Western leaders in particular declared that only through inflation—which would allow farmers to pay off loans more cheaply than when they had been negotiated, for the value of the currency they were returning would now be worth less—could agricultural problems be resolved. Warned that an amendment endorsing inflation, sponsored by Democratic Senator Elmer Thomas of Oklahoma, was going to be passed, Roosevelt, who saw the benefits of inflation himself, agreed to accept it as long as it gave him discretionary, rather than mandatory, powers to deal with currency. To appease conservatives, FDR indicated that he would appoint business executive George Peek, president of the Moline Plow Company, to head the new agency that would be created. While the promise made political sense, it caused administrative chaos, for Peek opposed the very efforts to cut back on production that the bill endorsed.

On May 12, Congress passed the Agricultural Adjustment Act, creating a new Agricultural Adjustment Administration (AAA), one of the most visible of the dozens of alphabet agencies that were part of the New Deal. Because it had taken some time to pass the measure, the farming season was already underway. Reluctantly, Wallace authorized the slaughter of about 6 million piglets and 200 thousand sows, and the plowing under of 10 million acres of cotton to make sure higher prices would be paid. In the face of public opposition to killing the baby pigs, he remarked, "I suppose it is a marvelous tribute to the humanitarian instincts of the American people that they sympathize more with little pigs which are killed than with full-grown hogs. Some people may object to killing pigs at any age. Perhaps, they think that farmers should run a sort of old-folks home for hogs and keep them around indefinitely as barnyard pets." While these actions were economically appropriate, they troubled people who deplored the destruction of good food in a country where millions were hungry and struggling to survive.

As the debate about the AAA dragged on, Roosevelt's interest in inflation led him to take a related step. On

April 19, he announced that he had taken the United States off the gold standard. That was heretical to purists who believed that all paper currency had to have the backing of a fixed amount of gold. The issue had been the source of huge controversy in the 1880s and 1890s, when Populists and their allies had demanded that silver, too, provide the backing for American currency. By refusing to be bound by the international price of gold, FDR had greater freedom to take action to raise domestic prices in an effort to stabilize the American economy.

Public generation of power was another issue that attracted Roosevelt's attention. Progressives had long been interested in providing for government control of an electric-power and nitrogen-development operation built during the Great War along the Tennessee River in the Muscle Shoals area in Alabama. Senator George Norris of Nebraska had been in the forefront of the effort, and twice Congress had passed such a measure, only to see it vetoed by Republicans in the White House. In January, before taking office, FDR had visited the area with Norris. As they left, reporters asked Norris, "Is he really with you?" Norris replied, "He is more than with me, because he plans to go even farther than I did." On April 10, Roosevelt asked Congress to create what would be called the Tennessee Valley Authority (TVA) to generate and distribute power, provide flood control through more dams, produce fertilizers, curb soil erosion, and offer services to improve health and education in the region. Not everyone was happy with the idea. One opponent, Representative Joe Martin of Massachusetts, charged that the TVA was "patterned closely after one of the soviet dreams." Such criticism notwithstanding, it was a bold and imaginative vision that entailed broad-based social and economic planning. On May 18, Congress created the TVA to facilitate development in an important part of the South.

Finally, FDR knew that he had to take immediate action to do something about industrial recovery. Initially, he recognized the same lack of consensus among business interests that he had encountered in the agricultural arena, and he and Moley decided to wait to see how thinking developed. Then, in early April, he learned that the Senate had just passed a bill, introduced by Senator Hugo Black of Alabama, providing for a 30-hour work week and banning from interstate commerce any goods produced where employees worked more than six hours a day or more than five days a week. The measure, Black asserted, would create six million jobs.

Roosevelt was concerned. He believed that the bill was unconstitutional and, furthermore, that it was too rigid and could not work in many of the industries he knew best. In the dairy business, he told Frances Perkins, there was no way to adapt the proposal for shortening the workday "to the rhythm of the cow." Worst of all, the measure would hurt workers by reducing their paychecks, since they would be working fewer hours, unless wages could be maintained. But the House was likely to pass the bill, and Roosevelt was reluctant to veto a piece of recovery legislation endorsed by many members of his own party. He recognized that it would be better to provide an alternative to the Black bill.

As with agriculture, numerous proposals lay on the table. Some businessmen wanted government to suspend antitrust laws to provide trade associations with the opportunity to work together collaboratively. Some looked back to the War Industries Board established during the Great War to facilitate government coordination of the massive recovery effort without undermining the capitalist system. Senator Robert Wagner insisted that if business was to be given such latitude, labor needed affirmation of rights long denied.

In mid-May, FDR sent Congress a multifaceted proposal that became the National Industrial Recovery Act (NIRA). Passed quickly by the House, more slowly by the Senate, it became law with Roosevelt's signature on June 16. The act contained something for everyone. It created the National Recovery Administration (NRA), which was to monitor the development of codes in each industry in the United States. Such codes, exempt from antitrust statutes, would mandate minimum wages and maximum hours and would also endorse reforms such as better working conditions and an end to child labor that union leaders had sought for decades. And the act contained the crucial Section 7(a), which guaranteed industrial workers the right "to organize and bargain collectively through representatives of their own choosing." To head the new agency, Roosevelt appointed Hugh Johnson, an occasional member of the "brain trust" and a protégé of Bernard Baruch, a wealthy financier who made a practice of advising presidents and a veteran of the War Industries Board.

The NIRA also addressed the need for public works. It created a Public Works Administration (PWA) to oversee a massive public construction program to build dams, bridges, and other structures and, in the process, provide jobs for unemployed Americans. Secretary of the Interior Harold Ickes took charge of the new agency, with an initial authorization of $3.3 billion, a huge sum at that time.

Signing the bill, Roosevelt declared: "Many good men voted this new charter with misgivings. I do not share these doubts. I had part in the great cooperation of 1917 and 1918 and it is my faith that we can count on our industry once more to join in our general purpose to lift this new threat." In his second fireside chat, he called the NRA "a partnership in planning" allowing business and government to work together, and explained to people huddled around their radios how the new system would work.

That same day, as it was about to adjourn, Congress completed work on a number of other measures. Just a short while before, it had passed the Securities Act, which directed the Federal Trade Commission to oversee issues of new securities. Now it approved the Glass-Steagall Banking Act, which separated commercial and investment banking and also provided federal insurance of bank deposits, to protect investors if another banking crisis ever occurred. Though FDR initially opposed the insurance provision, he recognized that it had significant popular support and, in the end, helped strengthen the banking system. Congress also approved a bill creating a Farm Credit Administration that, under the leadership of Roosevelt's friend Henry Morgenthau, Jr., combined a number of farm loan agencies to make it easier for farmers to borrow money, and a railroad regulation law.

The first hundred days were overwhelming. As he signed the last measures sent to him by Congress, Roosevelt observed that "more history is being made today than in [any] one day of our national life." By any standard, this was an extraordinary period. Roosevelt had delivered 10 speeches, sent 15 messages to Congress, and worked closely with legislators to guide 15 laws through to passage. The New Deal had dealt successfully with the banking crisis, reached out to the unemployed, established a program to help farmers, embarked on a new experiment in business-government cooperation, established a public works program, and more. Though the Great Depression still dragged on, millions of Americans now shared Roosevelt's sense of hope and optimism that the steps taken would help bring the return of prosperity. Journalist Walter Lippmann wrote: "At the end of February, we were a congeries of disorderly panic-stricken mobs and factions. In the hundred days from March to June we became again an organized nation confident of our power to provide for our own security and to control our own destiny."

Roosevelt himself seemed like a different man. Norman H. Davis, who had served as assistant secretary of the treasury under Wilson, observed to a friend, "That fellow in there is not the fellow we used to know. There's been a miracle here." Oswald Garrison Villard, editor of the magazine *The Nation*, wrote, "Many of us who have known him long and well ask ourselves if this is the same man." In fact, FDR had always had a steely resolve, even if it was not always visible to those around him. In the face of crisis, he had moved beyond what some critics saw as a glib shallowness and now showed an aggressive—and effective—sense of purpose. As Arthur Krock of the *New York Times* noted, "The President is the boss, the dynamo, the works."

Roosevelt presided over the White House with energy and enthusiasm. He had finally learned how to use his amiability to achieve his political ends. If he sometimes went off in a variety of directions at once, that simply gave him the time he needed to make up his own mind. For the duration of his presidency, he was often hard to pin down but only because he wanted to maintain his flexibility and to preserve his ability to act.

He frequently masked his own intentions, and he consciously sought to avoid labels. "I am that kind of a liberal," he remarked, "because I am that kind of a conservative." Asked once, "What is your philosophy?" he responded, "Philosophy? Philosophy? I am a Christian and a Democrat—that's all." When Eleanor pressed him early in their relationship to articulate what he thought about God and the teachings of the church, he answered, "I think it is just as well not to think about things like that too much." While he never subscribed to a fully-formulated set of personal beliefs, he nonetheless operated with a

Americans applauded FDR's jaunty outlook. Even his appearance, as in this picture of him in his car, conveyed his confidence.

powerful sense of purpose. Above all, he wanted to provide a measure of security for less fortunate citizens in the many sectors of American life. And he believed, as Endicott Peabody had taught him years before, that it was his task to serve God's purpose as best he could.

If he occasionally appeared vague about his plans for dealing with the Depression, part of that was his administrative style. His sometimes meandering approach reflected his effort to try first one thing, then another, to find a solution that worked. It was also his own way of avoiding organized opposition before he was ready to take decisive action. If his casual method worried aides, they came to understand that it was simply his way of operating. They had no choice but to go along.

Roosevelt prided himself on being able to do several things at once. Years before, while he was working on his stamp collection and listening to his mother read a story to him at the same time, she became annoyed when she thought he was not paying attention. He repeated back what she had just read, then said that he would "be ashamed if I couldn't do at least two things at once." Much later he told Henry Morgenthau, his Dutchess County neighbor and friend who became secretary of the treasury, "You know, I am a juggler, and I never let my right hand know what my left hand does." When Morgenthau asked, "Which hand am I, Mr. President?" FDR replied, "My right hand, but I keep my left hand under the table." He was, Morgenthau concluded, "a man of bewildering complexity of moods and motives."

Roosevelt was not troubled when his advisers had differences. Indeed, on a number of occasions, he told aides with diametrically opposed views to go into a room and not to come back until they had worked out a consistent position. Such had been the case during the 1932 campaign, as he looked ahead to hammering out a policy for agriculture, and said, "I am going to call farmers' leaders together, lock them in a room, and tell them not to come out until they have agreed on a plan," which is basically what he did. Such was also the case when it was necessary to come up with a draft of the NIRA.

At other times, FDR was content to allow open disagreements between agencies or advisers. "There is something to be said . . . for having a little conflict between agencies," he once declared. "A little rivalry is stimulating, you know. It keeps everybody going to prove that he is a better fellow than the next man." It allowed him to procrastinate when he chose, to watch his subordinates thrash out the details of an issue, and then to intervene when he was ready, with the ultimate power of decision in his own hands.

He also had a superb sense of timing, visible in the first hundred days, and even more evident as his presidency progressed. He could wait, indefinitely if necessary, until the right time to act. He was willing to confer with members of his administration, supposedly to discuss matters as yet undecided, only to ramble on genially about other issues for the entire meeting. Marriner Eccles, who became chairman of the Federal Reserve Board, once recalled how an important meeting never got started, for Roosevelt spent the entire time playing with his little dog Fala and then scolding the Scotch terrier for "purging himself on the rug." Eccles was furious until he finally realized that this was Roosevelt's way of avoiding difficult situations until he felt it was time to act.

With a wonderful sense of exuberance, Roosevelt gave notice from the very start that he intended to deal aggressively with the Great Depression. Just as the presidency had been a "bully pulpit" for TR, it was "pre-eminently a place of moral leadership" for FDR. At the end of the first hundred days, he had the legislation to address at least some of the nation's intractable economic and social problems. Now he had to make the new laws work.

5

New Deal Initiatives

During the first hundred days, Roosevelt's numerous initiatives created a basic framework for reviving the nation. Now the new agencies that were already swelling the size of the federal government had to begin the long, slow process of taking action. Tens of thousands of young lawyers and administrators flocked to Washington, D.C., to help participate in the lively and spirited effort that often seemed to be going in a variety of different directions at once. Relief programs provided needed assistance to the unemployed, and initiatives in the agricultural arena made life easier for many farmers. Yet efforts to jumpstart the economy failed to work effectively, and recovery remained elusive. Roosevelt, who had originally sought to take a balanced approach that appealed to all groups, found himself frustrated by critics on both the left and right sides of the political spectrum and, in time, rather than trying to please everyone, concentrated instead on working with those elements that could provide support for the necessary next steps.

Economic revival remained a top priority, and the NRA was the intended instrument of recovery. General Hugh Johnson, Roosevelt's choice to lead the new agency, was a gruff and tough manager, an energetic man with a lined, leathery face and a propensity for drinking too much and lashing out at critics too loudly. His colorful invective ensured that the NRA would be highly visible as he sought to reverse the downward business cycle. Disappointed that he was not going to have control over the public-works program, which he felt was an integral part of the recovery effort, he nonetheless understood the magnitude of the task he faced. "It will be red fire at first and dead cats afterward," he declared colorfully, if not clearly. "This is just like mounting the guillotine on the infinitesimal gamble that the ax won't work." Financier Bernard Baruch, who had worked with Johnson in the past, worried whether his friend was up to the task and told Frances Perkins: "I think he's a good number-three man, maybe a number-two man, but he's not a number-one man. He's dangerous and unstable. He gets nervous and sometimes goes away for days without notice. I'm fond of him, but do tell the President to be careful."

The NRA sought to eliminate cutthroat competition that was undermining the fragile economic system. FDR wanted Johnson to create a rational system of planning to stabilize the chaotic arrangements that had grown up haphazardly and no longer worked. Codes of fair practices in each industry would mandate appropriate wages, working conditions, and even prices and production levels. "The murderous doctrine of savage and wolfish competition, looking to dog-eat-dog and devil take the hindmost," Johnson said, had led employers to cut wages and lay off workers, thereby eroding purchasing power and eliminating a market for their products. For him, "the very heart of the New Deal is the principle of concerted action in industry and agriculture under government supervision," and he was determined to help bring it about.

Johnson's task became more difficult when he decided not to dictate what the codes should be but rather to negotiate the provisions with business and labor leaders in each industry. After quickly working out a cotton code for the textile industry, the process bogged down, and Johnson had difficulty persuading the nation's largest industries to cooperate. So he embarked on an aggressive propaganda effort to enlist their support. Drawing on lessons from the Great War, when the Committee on Public Information had whipped up sentiment against the horrible Hun, he launched a public-relations campaign to reward cooperative merchants and manufacturers. If they agreed to commit themselves to a standard code, they could then display a symbol showing their compliance—a Blue Eagle—with the slogan "We Do Our Part," as a way of encouraging consumers to deal with such businesses. Johnson designed the Blue Eagle image himself, basing it on a Native American thunderbird design. The president launched the campaign with another fireside chat in July, telling his radio listeners that "those who cooperate in this program must know each other at a glance. That is why we have provided a badge of honor for this purpose." There would be no coercion, he told them. Instead "opinion and conscience" would be "the only instruments we shall use in this great summer offensive against unemployment." Johnson was more outspoken: "May God have mercy on the man or group of men who attempt to trifle with this bird."

The Blue Eagle was everywhere. It appeared on posters and on billboards. Speakers spread the message during intermissions at movie theaters and asked for public support on street corners. In the summer of 1933, in the largest parade in New York City's history, about 200,000 people marched together down Fifth Avenue on behalf of the Blue Eagle. Not everyone approved of the glitzy campaign. Auto maker Henry Ford reportedly said, "Hell, that Roosevelt buzzard! I wouldn't put it on the car."

In a desperate effort to get industries to accept the codes, Johnson relied on trade associations to produce the desired results. Such organizations as the Iron and Steel Institute and the National Automobile Chamber of Commerce played a major role in drafting agreements for their industries. As a result, the largest companies in each industry were best represented and were able to call the shots. The NRA had both a Labor Board and a Consumer Advisory Board, but their voices were seldom heard as business interests predominated.

The whole effort was a bureaucratic nightmare. More than 700 different codes regulated everything from the dog-food industry to the burlesque theatrical industry, which specified no more than four stripteases in a given performance. Hardware stores had to pay close attention to 19 different codes, corkmakers to 34 different sets of regulations. An NRA staff of about 4,500 employees was constantly busy with thousands of interpretive rulings.

The NRA stabilized some chaotic industries, but at the expense of promoting the growth of monopoly as industries collaborated with one another in setting up the codes. Worse, it never managed to bring about the long-sought recovery. The codes, with their rigid stipulations, led business interests to cut back on production as a way of maintaining prices, but those cuts encouraged further layoffs and discouraged much-needed new investment.

The NRA did have an impact on union organizing. Some labor leaders used Section 7(a) of the original NIRA legislation as a mandate for unionization. John L. Lewis, the vigorous and vociferous leader of the United Mine Workers (UMW), was in the forefront of the effort in 1933, as he dispatched organizers to tell workers, "The President wants you to unionize." Within a year the UMW, which had shrunk to about 150,000 members, grew to more than 500,000. But some employers, notably those in the automobile and steel industries, found they could comply with the mandate of Section 7(a) by forming company unions, which they could control, and which hardly served the interests of their employees.

By early 1934, people could be heard complaining about "NRA prices and Hoover wages." Some labor leaders said that the initials NRA stood for "National Run Around." Newspaper magnate William Randolph Hearst claimed they stood for "No Recovery Allowed." In the fall of the year, as complaints became more vocal and Johnson's behavior became more erratic, FDR secured Johnson's resignation, though the president was not yet ready to give up on the entire recovery effort. The original legislation had specified a two-year life span for the NRA. Despite its inability to achieve the desired results, Roosevelt remained hopeful that it could work effectively. In early 1935, he therefore asked Congress for a two-year extension, saying, "The fundamental purposes and principles of the Act are sound. To abandon them is unthinkable. It would spell the return of industrial and labor chaos." In May of that year, before Congress could act, the Supreme Court ruled unanimously in the case of *Schechter Poultry Corp.* v. *United States* that the NRA was based on "an unconstitutional delegation of legislative power"; with that ruling it ceased to function. Roosevelt accepted the result reluctantly. "You know the whole thing is a mess," he told Frances Perkins. "It has been an awful headache. . . . I think perhaps the NRA has done all it can do."

Nor did the PWA, which was left intact by the *Schechter* ruling, have much of an impact on recovery. An aggressive public-works program had the potential to stimulate the economy, but not the way Harold Ickes ran it. Well aware of the scandals in the Interior Department in the preceding administration, he was determined to avoid even the hint of impropriety. When his name as the possible director first surfaced at a cabinet meeting, he remarked, "This is so sudden, Mr. President, but I think I have at least the negative and austere qualities which the handling of so much public money requires." His self-assessment was correct, and he soon came to be called "Honest Harold" for the painfully slow way he allocated PWA funds. His meticulous attention to detail bogged down the entire spending process. As one of his assistants said in frustration, "He still has to learn that the Administrator of a $3 billion fund hasn't the time to check every typewriter acquisition." But Ickes persisted in running the PWA his own way, spending only $110 million of the initial allocation in 1933 and accomplishing his aim "of administering the greatest fund for construction in the history of the world without scandal." The slow, deliberate pace notwithstanding, he deserved credit for the structures the PWA produced. Between 1933 and 1939, the agency was responsible for building a vast number of important projects—the Triborough Bridge and the Lincoln Tunnel in New York City, and the Grand Coulee, Boulder, and Bonneville Dams in the West, to mention but a few. It also helped build 70 percent of the nation's new school buildings and 65 percent of its city halls, sewage treatment plants, and courthouses. In that way it helped bolster the nation's infrastructure. But it might have helped stimulate recovery as well, had it been given the chance.

The Reconstruction Finance Corporation was more active in promoting recovery at the start. It was established toward the end of Hoover's administration, and Roosevelt recognized its possibilities and let it play a larger role than before. He appointed Jesse Jones, a Texas banker, as head. Under his leadership, the agency bought bank stock as a way of increasing banks' capital base, thereby allowing them to extend the credit they offered. The idea was to bolster their stability as they reentered credit markets. The RFC effectively became the nation's largest bank, helped support a variety of federal mortgage agencies and other lending institutions, and in that way sought to stimulate the stagnant economy.

The effort to revive agriculture was closely related to the larger recovery effort. Secretary of Agriculture Henry Wallace was a passionate administrator intent on reviving the farming sector. He was a prominent geneticist who had made a name for himself breeding hybrid corn, but was at the same time a man of many interests, a rumpled and rustic man of the soil, someone in novelist Sherwood Anderson's phrase with "no swank," a dreamy mystic given to periodic flights of fancy. He lived a simple life, rising early, walking to work, refusing tobacco, liquor, and sometimes meat, on occasion subsisting on soybeans and cottonseed meal instead. He was a deeply religious man who felt close to what he called "that blissful unmanifested reality which we call God" and was moved by stories of the Old Testament prophets. Yet his practical side helped him understand what had to be done to help American farmers.

Wallace was committed to the domestic allotment plan that sought to curb overproduction by offering farmers government payments not to grow crops as a way of raising prices. In the summer of 1933, some farmers, led by the articulate Milo Reno, head of the Farmers' Holiday Association, and Floyd Olson, the radical governor of Minnesota and leader of the state's upstart Farmer-Labor Party, demanded mandatory production controls and fixed prices. When Wallace and Roosevelt refused to accede to a compulsory approach, the Farmers' Holiday Association responded in November with a strike in which activists destroyed dairies and cheese factories, poured kerosene into cream, and dumped milk on highways. Though the violence against property finally abated, demands for mandatory controls did not, and the next year Congress passed the Bankhead Cotton Control Act and the Kerr-Smith Tobacco Control Act, and later still a Potato Control Act.

Another part of the effort to restrict production was by providing the incentives of a loan program. In the fall of 1933, Jesse Jones established a Commodity Credit Corporation, to lend money to farmers willing to take land out of production the following year. With loan rates better than the market price, the program served as a kind of long-range price support for those able to look ahead to the future.

In its first year, the Agricultural Adjustment Administration worked reasonably well in raising prices. Cotton prices jumped from under 7 cents a pound to more than 12 cents a pound in 1934, while wheat rose from 38 cents a bushel to 86 cents and corn increased from 32 cents a bushel to 82 cents in the same period. There was similar progress in the longer term: Over the course of FDR's first four years in office, total farm income rose about 50 percent.

But there were unintended consequences. The AAA worked through Extension Service agents, who had ties to farmers in most rural counties. The agents established local production-control committees to administer the AAA programs, and gravitated toward the large commercial farmers with whom they had worked most closely in the past. As the program unfolded, large landowners accepted government payments for not planting crops, and then pushed sharecroppers and tenant farmers—black and white—off the land being withheld from cultivation, while continuing to farm other parts of the land themselves. Although the AAA was supposed to help tenants and sharecroppers get a fair share of government money, it seldom worked that way. One result was the creation of the Southern Tenant Farmers' Union in 1934, to try to secure better treatment for those farmers who owned no land.

Sharecroppers, who did not own their own land but paid for the right to farm by paying the owner a portion of each season's crop, had a particularly hard time. Many of them worked in the cotton South, where they had to purchase tools, seed, and supplies from the landlord and, because of the exorbitant prices he charged, never managed to get out of debt or escape their plight. The system, which included about a million white and half a million black households, left the participants in abject poverty. Journalist Lorena Hickok observed that they "seemed to belong to another land than the America I knew and loved." Author James Agee and photographer Walker Evans provided a powerful report on conditions in Alabama in their sobering book *Let Us Now Praise Famous Men*.

Victims of the Dust Bowl likewise suffered more than most. Farmers in the Great Plains, in the region centered on Oklahoma and surrounding states, had cut through the sod to plant ever more crops without concern for the topsoil that ran off when the rains came. A devastating drought that began in 1932 brought with it dust storms that blocked visibility for miles around. About a million "Okies" left their homes in search of better conditions elsewhere, often on the West Coast. Photographer Dorothea Lange and her husband Paul Shuster Taylor documented their suffering in *An American Exodus: A Record of Human Erosion* in 1938, while John Steinbeck described their lives vividly in his story of the Joad family in his novel *The Grapes of Wrath*, which appeared the next year.

There was also internal strife in the AAA. Roosevelt had appointed as head of the agency George Peek, a gruff, testy, pugnacious veteran of the fight to help the farmers in the 1920s. Peek wanted to allow farmers to produce as much as they could and then dump the surplus abroad.

"The job's simple," he said. "It's just to put up farm prices." He therefore basically disagreed with the AAA program he was required to implement. He found himself up against a liberal faction headed by Rexford Tugwell, now assistant secretary of agriculture, and Jerome Frank, general counsel of the department. Peek had no use for such intellectuals—"boys with their hair ablaze" he called them—who wanted to assist the sharecroppers and ensure that consumers were not ignored in favor of the largest producers. As the conflict became intolerable, Roosevelt recognized he had to act. In mid-December 1933, he eased Peek out of the AAA by designating him special adviser on foreign trade. The young radicals had more of a voice for a time but, in the end, Wallace circumscribed their efforts in what he felt were the interests of the larger program. As he later explained, "Well, you see we don't like to have a ship that lists stronger to the left or the right, but one that goes straight ahead." He intended to subsidize the farmer without fixing prices, to limit production through a voluntary approach, and to resist dumping surpluses abroad. And though that approach worked reasonably well, it took time to produce lasting results.

Faced early in his term with agitated farmers who wanted inflation to help them deal with their debts, Roosevelt knew he had to do something to respond to the crisis. He had already taken the United States off the gold standard and, in mid-1933, he sent word to an International Economic Conference in London that the United States would refuse to work collaboratively to stabilize currencies, for he wished to deal with the American economy on his own.

He came up with a curious plan. A number of economists persuaded him that if the federal government purchased gold at increasing prices, that action would have the effect of devaluing the dollar, for it would increase the number of dollars necessary to buy each ounce of gold. It would thereby stop the slide of falling prices, and provide the inflation the farmers in particular wanted. Roosevelt later contended that "if we had continued a week or so longer without my having made this move on gold, we would have had an agricultural revolution in this country." And so, each morning, FDR met with Henry Morgenthau, now secretary of the treasury, and Jesse Jones to decide on the price for the day. The process was hardly scientific. One morning, Roosevelt decided on an increase of 21 cents, reasoning that "it's a lucky number, because it's three times seven." Morgenthau, much more serious about the practice, noted in his diary, "If anybody knew how we really set the gold price through a combination of lucky numbers, etc., I think they would be frightened." English economist John Maynard Keynes was even more critical. The scheme, he declared, "looked to me more like a gold standard on the booze than the ideal managed currency of my dreams."

The gold-buying plan failed to work. Domestic commodity prices, in fact, fell somewhat at the end of 1933. In January 1934, Roosevelt suspended the scheme. It had satisfied his eagerness to take action—any kind of action—and it had bought time to allow some of the farm programs to begin to work. But it was one of the various initiatives that failed to bring about the desired recovery of the economy.

To be sure, reviving the economic system was not the only priority. Roosevelt recognized the pressing need to help millions of desperate Americans who had lost their jobs and had nowhere to turn. Not only were some people starving, but many more had lost hope. In the United States, with its long tradition of individualism, people had persuaded themselves that they were personally responsible for whatever success they enjoyed. That attitude worked well enough in the prosperous 1920s, but with the collapse of the economic system in the 1930s, people felt failure was their own responsibility. A sense of shame compounded their desperation. Men, traditionally the breadwinners of the family, now found themselves unable to put food on the table, and that inability undermined their stature with wives and children and eroded their self-esteem. Women tried to pick up some of the slack, but that effort sometimes exacerbated family tensions. In countless letters addressed to either Franklin or Eleanor Roosevelt—or to them both—poverty-stricken Americans poured out their hearts and pleaded for help. An anonymous letter from Chicago summed up one family's plight: "I am a boy of 12 years old. I want to tell you about my family. My father hasn't worked for 5 months. . . . My father he staying home. All the time he's crying because he can't find work. I told him why are you crying daddy, and daddy said why shouldn't I cry when there is nothing in the house." Another man from Latrobe, Pennsylvania, wrote about his inability to support his wife and six children and asked, "Can you be so kind as to advise me as to which would be the most human way to dispose of my self and my family, as this is about the only thing that I see left to do."

Harry Hopkins spearheaded the relief effort. The son of an Iowa harness maker, he had worked one summer when he was a college student in Christadora House, a settlement house in New York City, and that experience launched him on a career in social work. But Hopkins did not seem like a typical social worker or a typical New Dealer. As much as he was committed to helping people in need, he still enjoyed escaping that grim world by going to the race track and betting on horses. A man of enormous nervous energy, he was a chain smoker and consumer of endless cups of coffee. He always seemed disheveled, and his language was sometimes profane. According to one observer, "He gives off a suggestion of quick cigarettes, thinning hair, dandruff, brief sarcasm, fraying suits of clothes, and a wholly understandable preoccupation." More than most, he understood what Roosevelt wanted, and had, as Raymond Moley once noted, a "capacity for quick and, it should be added, expensive activity." His organizational ability led British statesman Winston Churchill to later call him "Lord Root of the Matter."

Almost immediately after his appointment as head of the Federal Emergency Relief Administration, Hopkins set up a desk in the hallway of the Reconstruction Finance Corporation building and began writing checks. In his first two hours he spent more than $5 million. Relief was not direct, but needed to be channeled through local public agencies. By October, Hopkins had spent his entire $500 million allocation without having made a major dent in the problem. He found himself dissatisfied with the makeshift relief effort and troubled with the means test used by local administrators to determine who was worthy of assistance. With the approach of winter, something more was needed, and Hopkins wanted to try a new work-relief approach. Having something to do in exchange for financial assistance, he argued, "preserves a man's morale. It saves his skill. It gives him something socially useful to do." He persuaded Roosevelt to establish a temporary work-relief program consisting of small projects until the Public Works Administration began to act more aggressively. The new Civil Works Administration (CWA), working with an allocation from the PWA budget, placed people on the federal payroll.

The CWA was successful. In its first month, it hired 2.6 million workers, and by January 1934, it had 4.2 million on the payroll. Half of them came from relief rolls; the other half were simply needy people who could be appointed without having to take a humiliating means test. The CWA paid people an average of more than $15 a week, a modest amount, but two-and-a-half times what the FERA had paid. It built half a million miles of roads, as well as schools, playgrounds, and airports. It laid sewer lines, constructed bridges, and even built outhouses for farmers. It paid teachers in rural areas, so schools could be kept open, and also hired 3,000 writers and artists, so they could use their skills to support themselves. People were delighted. One woman in Iowa said, "The first thing I did was to go out and buy a dozen oranges. I hadn't tasted any for so long that I had forgotten what they were like." A man in Alabama, referring to his CWA card, told Lorena Hickok, "When I got that card, it was the biggest day in my whole life. At last I could say, 'I've got a job.'"

In the course of spending about $834 million over a period of five months, the CWA was popular with hired workers but drew mixed reactions from other quarters. Hopkins was satisfied. "Long after the workers of the CWA are dead and gone and these hard times forgotten," he declared, "their effort will be remembered by permanent useful works in every county of every state." But there was inevitable waste, which attracted criticism, and Roosevelt was worried that it was too costly and could create a permanent class of relief recipients. If it continued into the summer, he told his staff, it could "become a habit with the country." And so, in the spring of 1934, he ordered the dismantling of the CWA and mandated that the FERA resume its relief efforts.

By the end of the year, FDR was finally ready to move forward more boldly with a new relief initiative. As the Depression dragged on, more and more people were added to the welfare rolls, so that approximately 20 million people were now receiving pubic assistance of some sort. A more aggressive work-relief program, whatever the cost, he concluded, was probably preferable. To that end, he proposed a massive new appropriation for emergency public employment that would hire 3.5 million people. He requested $4.88 billion—$4 billion in new money and $880 million in reallocations from earlier appropriations—in what was at the time the largest single appropriation in the nation's history. The Emergency Relief Appropriation Act, passed by Congress in April 1935, gave Roosevelt considerable autonomy in allocating a huge amount of money. It also created a new agency, the Works Progress Administration (WPA), to be headed by Harry Hopkins.

Roosevelt used his authority to channel funds where he chose. Some money went to older organizations, such as the CCC, while some supported new agencies, such as the Rural Electrification Administration and the National Youth Administration. But the real competition for funds pitted Harry Hopkins against Harold Ickes, administrator of the PWA. The two men were hardly fond of one another. Ickes felt that Hopkins was not interested in priming the pump to revive the economy but "just turning on the fire plug." Hopkins, in turn, was impatient with the slow pace of the PWA and called Ickes "the 'great resigner'—anything doesn't go his way, threatens to quit. He bores me." In the end, with his intention of putting as many people as possible to work as quickly as he could, Hopkins persuaded FDR to give him the largest allocation.

FDR took pride as the WPA became one of the most visible programs of the New Deal. It built thousands of schools, hospitals, playgrounds and airfields. It restored old buildings, such as the Dock Theater in Charleston, South Carolina, and built new ones, such as Timberline Lodge on Oregon's Mount Hood. Critics complained about makework projects, like leaf raking, and claimed that in some cases one crew dug a hole, and then another filled it in, but if such projects existed, they were just a small part of the overall program. The WPA also showed tremendous creativity in putting all kinds of skilled professionals to work. There was, for example, a Federal Art Project, which hired artists such as Willem De Kooning and Jackson Pollock to paint and teach art and appointed other artists who drew on the example of Mexican muralist Diego Rivera to produce murals, often with radical themes, at sites around the country. When the art project came under attack as frivolous, Hopkins defended the decision to help support artists by saying, "Hell, they've got to eat just like other people." Roosevelt found some of the murals good, "some not so good," but understood the energy and vitality in the images. A Federal Theatre Project paid actors and directors to mount stage productions, old and new, some even in languages like Yiddish and French. Orson Welles, not yet twenty years old when appointed as a Federal Theatre Project director, staged a production of William Shakespeare's *Macbeth* with an all-black cast. A Federal Writers' Project hired established authors, such as Conrad Aiken, as well as new writers, such as John Cheever and Richard Wright. Writers worked on the American Guide Series, producing books about all of the nation's states as well as 150 volumes in a "Life in America" series. They moved into other areas as well, as in the effort to record the recollections of former slaves before they died. And a Federal Music Project paid a living wage to about 15,000 musicians who gave concerts and recorded traditional rural American songs.

The WPA was a remarkable undertaking. Though it hardly dealt with all of the unemployed in America, it put a significant number of people back to work and helped the nation look back at its past as it struggled to extricate itself from the worst economic crisis it had ever known.

At the start of the New Deal, Roosevelt was concerned with balancing competing interests. Recognizing fundamental imbalances in the old order, he wanted to work with a wide variety of different groups to create a new equilibrium in both industry and agriculture. He hoped to avoid partisan conflict in the effort to revive the capitalist system and to make it functional again. He was prepared to work with farmers and farm leaders as well as with businessmen and business leaders in the recovery effort. Sometimes that approach proved difficult as disagreements invariably surfaced. Staff members dedicated to balancing the budget often clashed with those intent on providing relief for suffering Americans. Farmers were suspicious of businessmen who played a major role in the NRA, while businessmen were uncomfortable with New Deal programs they deemed too radical. It was not easy for FDR to maintain a middle course in his effort to be, like the Wizard of Oz, all things to all people.

It became even more difficult as the recovery effort bogged down and opposition groups began to coalesce. By the summer of 1934, about a year-and-a-half after taking office, with the economy still in the doldrums, Roosevelt began to worry about growing resistance on a number of fronts.

Conservatives, many of them members of the Democratic Party, were infuriated by the direction of the New Deal and responded by establishing the American Liberty League. R. R. M. Carpenter, a retired official with the Du Pont corporation, started the process by complaining to John J. Raskob, a top-ranking Du Pont official who had also served as chairman of the Democratic Party, that "five Negroes on my place in South Carolina refused work this Spring . . . saying they had easy jobs with the government. . . . A cook on my houseboat at Fort Myers quit because the government was paying him a dollar an hour as a painter." Something clearly needed to be done, and for such critics the Liberty League was the answer. Its leaders included Raskob and Al Smith, former Democratic nominee for the presidency in 1928, while members included John W. Davis, Democratic presidential nominee in 1924, and corporate leaders like Alfred P. Sloan of General Motors and Sewell Avery of Montgomery Ward. Raskob declared that business needed to "organize to protect society from the suffering it is bound to endure if . . . no one should be allowed to get rich." Jouett Shouse, former chairman of the Democratic Executive Committee and now Liberty League chairman, observed that the new organization would "teach the necessity of respect for the rights of persons and property as fundamental to every successful form of government," and would resist "any measures designed to destroy the principles upon which our government was formulated and under which we have prospered as has no other nation in the history of the world."

Roosevelt was especially troubled by more visible critics who captured considerable public attention. Huey Long, the loud and colorful senator from Louisiana, posed the greatest threat. Raised in the rural South, he used populist rhetoric to appeal to poor farmers and industrial workers, and had run on the slogan "Every man a king, but no one wears a crown" when he won election as governor of Louisiana in 1928. In office, he challenged entrenched interests as he raised taxes on producers of oil and gas and used the money to improve schools, hospitals, and other public services, all at a substantial cost in graft and dictatorial control. Then, in 1932, he was elected to the Senate and went to Washington, with his eye on the presidency. He supported FDR during the campaign, but broke with him soon after Roosevelt took office.

Long was easily identifiable. He had a pug nose and a ruddy face that made him look like a cherub, and was fond of dressing flamboyantly in white silk suits, pink ties, and striped straw hats. He took on the nickname "Kingfish," after a scheming character on the popular radio program *Amos 'n' Andy*. The *New York Times* called him "a man with a front of brass and lungs of leather." Roosevelt himself referred to him as "one of the two most dangerous men in the country," the other being the arrogant but able Army Chief of Staff Douglas MacArthur.

In 1934, Long founded his Share Our Wealth Society. It was a clear challenge—and alternative—to the New Deal, which he complained "took four hundred millions from the soldiers and spent three hundred millions to plant saplings." Even worse, he declared, "Not a single thin dime of concentrated, bloated, pompous wealth, massed in the hands of a few people, has been raked down to relieve the masses." Long proposed liquidating large fortunes and using the money to give every American family about $5,000 to buy a home, a car, and a radio, and to guarantee a family income of $2,500, nearly twice the average at the time.

Although analysts demonstrated that the plan was not mathematically feasible, neither Long nor his followers worried about the details. By early 1935, there were more than 27,000 Share Our Wealth clubs, and a mailing list of 7.5 million people. Supporters included Northern workers and Western farmers in addition to Long's natural base in the South. A Democratic National Committee poll showed that he might gain three or four million votes as a third party candidate in 1936. The threat ended when Long was assassinated in September 1935.

Other critics of the New Deal were equally vocal. The Reverend Charles Coughlin, a Roman Catholic priest from Royal Oak, Michigan, had a national radio audience of between 30 and 45 million listeners by the end of 1932. One address that year, attacking Hoover as "the banker's friend, the Holy Ghost of the rich, the protective angel of Wall Street," attracted 1.2 million letters, while his regular mail averaged 80 thousand letters a week. In his rich and melodious voice, Father Coughlin castigated bankers as the source of the nation's problems, but condemned Communism as well. Initially, he supported FDR, but then declared that Roosevelt was not moving quickly enough to bring about needed inflation. Like the Populists in the late nineteenth century, he wanted silver to be a basis for currency, proclaiming at the end of 1933: "Forward to Christ all ye people! God wills it—this religious crusade against the pagan god of gold." For him, "Silver is the key to world prosperity."

Lashing out at the New Deal near the end of 1934, Coughlin formed the National Union for Social Justice. Capitalism was on its last legs, he asserted, and his system of social justice would take its place. While Coughlin was not a political threat, since his Canadian birth precluded a run for the presidency, Roosevelt worried about the implications if Coughlin supported Huey Long.

Still another critic was Dr. Francis Townsend. A retired physician living in Long Beach, California, he wrote a letter toward the end of 1933 to the editor of the *Long Beach Press-Telegram* outlining his own "Cure for Depressions." In it he argued that the government needed to pay attention to elderly people in any recovery scheme. When his letter received an overwhelming response that continued for the next several weeks, Townsend recognized he had to come up with details of a plan. To that end, he established an organization in early 1934 he called Old Age Revolving Pensions, Ltd.

His plan was simple. It promised a monthly pension of $200 for each American over the age of 60 who would agree to retire from all employment and to spend the money within one month. The payment would be financed by a

2 percent tax on business transactions that would be held in a "revolving fund."

Critics pointed out problems. The plan would require payment of $24 billion a year to 9 percent of the population, when the entire national income was only $40 billion. None of that mattered to followers. By Townsend's estimate, 25 million Americans had signed petitions in favor of his proposal; opponents acknowledged that he had gathered at least 10 million signatures. About 3.5 million people belonged to local clubs that were part of Townsend's organization. Townsend ignored the criticisms. When asked by the chairman of the House Ways and Means Committee about whether the tax he proposed would raise enough money, he responded, "I'm not in the least interested in the cost of the plan."

Another challenge came in the campaign for governor of California launched in the fall of 1933 by muckraking novelist Upton Sinclair. Calling his program EPIC—End Poverty in California—Sinclair, a noted Socialist, argued that idle workers should be allowed to produce food and goods for their own needs. The state, he proposed, should buy or lease land and rent idle factories to enable people to work on the basis of production-for-use. Entering the Democratic primary, Sinclair won a stunning victory, and seemed to have a good shot at winning the general election.

Though in the end Sinclair lost his bid to become governor of California, activists who applauded Roosevelt and wanted him to do even more made their voices heard in the midterm elections of 1934. While the party in power usually expects to lose congressional seats in such contests, the Democratic Party scored a huge victory. It won 26 of 35 races for the Senate, ending up with a 69–25 majority. It also gained seats in the House of Representatives and now held a 322–103 majority (with the rest of the seats in both houses belonging to Progressives and Farmer-Laborites).

People, even in areas that had been less supportive in 1932, approved the course the administration was taking and wanted it to continue.

Though Roosevelt was concerned about his critics, he remained tremendously popular. In a fireside chat in June 1934, he had asked people to "judge recovery" by "the plain facts of your individual situation. Are you better off than you were last year?" Although recovery remained elusive, he had the nation's voters in his camp. The midterm election was a stunning personal victory for the president, even without being on the ballot himself. As Kansas newspaper editor William Allen White observed, "He has been all but crowned by the people." Harry Hopkins was delighted. "This is our hour," he said. "We've got to get everything we want—now or never." FDR recognized the remarkable opportunity, but was also determined to act with caution. He understood that as his own party moved to the left, he needed to move along with it. But he also knew that he had to keep control of the party, and not move too far too fast.

The 1934 electoral victory emboldened Roosevelt to push ahead with a number of important initiatives in 1935. The massive relief effort that included the creation of the WPA was a major part of the program. But there were also other plans he had been considering for some time and was now ready to act upon.

The most important of those was a social security program. As governor of New York, Roosevelt had recognized the need for some kind of government sponsored social insurance. He was interested in unemployment insurance as well as in pensions for the elderly and he was determined to weave both elements into a comprehensive program. He had Frances Perkins firmly on his side, and she had told him of her intention of pushing ahead in this direction when he appointed her secretary of labor. As

Congress began to consider various alternatives of its own in early 1934, FDR asked Perkins to chair a committee to determine the best approach.

Roosevelt was aware of various precedents. Germany had established a compulsory social insurance scheme at the end of the nineteenth century, and other European countries had done likewise. In the United States, the Progressive Party—headed by TR—had called for old-age pensions in 1912, and Roosevelt himself had supported the idea when he met with other governors in 1930. The Democratic platform in 1932 similarly committed the party to "unemployment and old-age insurance under State laws."

Now Roosevelt began to consider an even more comprehensive approach. To Perkins, he argued that "there is no reason why everybody in the United States should not be covered. . . . I don't see why not. Cradle to the grave—from the cradle to the grave they ought to be in a social insurance system." But Roosevelt and Perkins both recognized that political realities required some limits. The committee Perkins convened understood not only the political constraints but also the constitutional issues involved. Though it would be easier and more practical to construct a single national system, it was necessary to keep some authority lodged with the states. And with a number of important New Deal programs—the AAA and the NRA—already facing court challenges that were working their way to the Supreme Court, a full-fledged national system might not pass the constitutional test.

A particularly prickly point involved workers' contributions. Roosevelt was adamant that "the funds necessary to provide this insurance should be raised by contribution rather than by an increase in general taxation." He stood by his support of payroll taxes. "No dole," he said, "mustn't have a dole." Years later, he reflected that "those taxes were never a problem of economics. They are politics all the way through. We put those payroll contributions there so as to give the contributors a legal, moral, and political right to collect their pensions and their unemployment benefits. With those taxes in there, no damn politician can ever scrap my social security program."

In mid-January 1935, Roosevelt asked Congress for the necessary social security legislation. In congressional hearings, conservatives lashed out at the plan. "It would take the romance out of life," New Jersey Senator A. Harry Moore declared. "We might as well take a child from the nursery, give him a nurse, and protect him from every experience that life affords." Yet with able congressional leadership, both the Senate and the House of Representatives passed the measure, and in August Roosevelt signed it into law.

The Social Security Act, which Perkins said Roosevelt always regarded as the "cornerstone of his administration," was a major step forward in the creation of a welfare state that would help those who could not help themselves. As the president wished, it provided for both unemployment insurance and old-age pensions, and covered about 26 million workers. It had limitations, to be sure. It was not all-inclusive. It relied on a payroll tax, to be initiated immediately, with the first pensions not to be paid for several years. But with what Perkins called "practical, flat-footed first steps," it was a start.

That same year, recognizing the need for reform, FDR finally threw his support behind a major piece of labor legislation. Senator Robert Wagner had long wanted to set up a National Labor Relations Board to conduct elections in which workers could choose the bargaining unit they wanted. That was a way to ensure that workers could bargain collectively, without being hindered by employers. Roosevelt, initially not particularly interested in labor issues, opposed Wagner's approach. But as the measure sailed through the Senate in May 1935, he saw that it was bound to pass and so shifted course and called it a piece of "must" legislation. At just about that time, the Supreme Court handed down its verdict in *Schechter*, ruling the NRA unconstitutional and eliminating its provisions for labor organizing. Now the National Labor Relations Act, or Wagner Act as it was commonly called, was even more important than before. After passage in the House of Representatives, FDR signed it in early July. There was now a firm grounding for unionization, which changed the state of labor-business relations in the United States.

FDR embarked on a number of other important initiatives in 1935. He set up the Resettlement Administration and asked Rexford Tugwell to head it, in an effort to deal with the problems of rural poverty. Interested in demonstrating the possibilities of urban planning, the agency also built three "greenbelt towns" that were near employment centers but surrounded by open countryside; one was near Washington, D.C., one near Cincinnati, and one near Milwaukee. Roosevelt established as well the Rural Electrification Administration, which played a major role in bringing electric power to the farm population. The Banking Act of 1935 gave the president more control over the Federal Reserve System and provided the Board of Governors, which he appointed, with greater authority over regional banks and money markets. The Wealth Tax of 1935 started off as a measure to redistribute national wealth, but was gutted in Congress, though it did end up raising estate, gift, and excess-profits taxes. And the Public Utilities Holding Company Act made it easier to break up the large power companies that fleeced the public and had long managed to evade regulation.

This flurry of activity in 1935, sometimes called the second hundred days, was another remarkable undertaking. During this period, Roosevelt moved ahead with programs already started and plans considered in the past, in his multitiered effort to deal with the ongoing problems of the Great Depression and to promote lasting social reform. As the electorate shifted to the left, FDR traveled in the same direction.

Success and Stalemate

As he presided over a wave of new initiatives in 1935, Roosevelt enjoyed widespread support. Huge Democratic majorities in both houses of Congress gave him the backing he needed for the legislative success of the New Deal, and he worked closely with allies on Capitol Hill to push through the bills he wanted. The relief effort was assisting millions of Americans who were now receiving government aid from a variety of new programs. They felt a bond with the president they had never known with any leader in the past, and that sense of affection for FDR revived a sense of confidence in the country, even if the United States remained mired in the Great Depression. But the Supreme Court, dominated by conservative justices, was already proving problematic, and the New Deal was in jeopardy if key measures failed to gain judicial approval. FDR knew he needed another term to consolidate his gains and to bring about recovery.

The level of personal support for him was overwhelming. After listening to Roosevelt on the radio, huge numbers of Americans wrote to the president voicing their approval of what he was doing. When, during one address, FDR asked listeners to "tell me your troubles," they responded right away. According to the White House chief of mail, the messages arrived so fast that "within a week I had some 450,000 letters stacked all over the office." Some were written on real stationery, others on scraps of paper. Louis Howe once commented on a recurring nightmare he had, in which he was "in an airplane, high up, so that the whole map of the United States lies spread out beneath me. . . . It appears to be covered with a white blanket flowing toward one point. As the airplane descends, I find to my horror that the white blanket consists of letters—letters from every part of the country—and their ultimate destination is the White House." Roosevelt regularly read a sampling of the letters, and his staff answered most of them.

Roosevelt had the capacity to make people feel that he understood their plight. One New Yorker who signed his letter "Hutch" wrote, after one radio address, "men were slapping each other on their backs and enthusiastically shaking hands in self congratulation that, at last, the public has a BUDDY in the White House." A man from Columbus, Georgia, wrote, "hoping that you'll excuse this, but I've always thought of F.D.R. as my personal friend." And another worker remarked, in perhaps the most telling comment of all, "Mr. Roosevelt is the only man we ever had in the White House who would understand that my boss is a son-of-a-bitch."

Eleanor, who traveled around the country and reported back to her husband, was also viewed as a friend. When another bonus army group came to Washington in 1933, she joined the ex-soldiers and led them in singing "There's a long, long trail a-winding." The contrast between her response and Hoover's could not have been more dramatic. She, too, got a huge amount of mail and other encouragement. A cartoon in the *New Yorker* showed a coal miner saying, "For gosh sakes, here comes Mrs. Roosevelt."

Looking toward reelection, FDR was confident of victory. "We will win easily next year," he told the cabinet in

November 1935, "but we are going to make it a crusade." The real question was whether or not to continue trying to work with the business community, as well as with a wide variety of other groups, or to strike out in a more partisan direction. Roosevelt remained undecided in the first few months of 1936, but by the middle of the year he began to move toward a decision as he became worried about Alf M. Landon, governor of Kansas and front runner for the Republican presidential nomination. Landon was a successful businessman who radiated competence and common sense and might well appeal to Americans ready to work even more closely than the government with corporate colleagues to end the Depression.

Meanwhile, Roosevelt was increasingly irritated by the growing opposition of businessmen to the efforts of the New Deal. On one occasion early in his first term, he had written to a Boston banker who had been a Harvard classmate and noted that he had heard about derogatory comments the man had made. FDR concluded that "because of what I felt to be to be a very old and real friendship these remarks hurt." A few years later, he was angrier when he told a story highlighting his disappointment with the business world, especially after he had bailed out the capitalist system and permitted it to survive: "In the summer of 1933, a nice old gentleman wearing a silk hat fell off the end of a pier. He was unable to swim. A friend ran down the pier, dived overboard and pulled him out; but the silk hat floated off with the tide. After the old gentleman had been revived, he was effusive in his thanks. He praised his friend for saving his life. Today, three years later, the old gentleman is berating his friend because the silk hat was lost."

Roosevelt observed in his annual message to Congress in January 1936 that "we have earned the hatred of entrenched greed," but he waited until his renomination in June to speak out more boldly. In Philadelphia, with 100,000 people in attendance at Franklin Field, he gave the outdoor crowd what it had come for, as he went on the attack against entrenched business interests. "These economic royalists," he proclaimed, "complain that we seek to overthrow the institutions of America. What they really complain of is that we seek to take away their power." As he came to the end of his remarks, he spoke with a commanding eloquence: "Governments can err, Presidents do make mistakes, but the immortal Dante tells us that divine justice weighs the sins of the cold-blooded and the sins of the warm-hearted in different scales. Better the occasional faults of a Government that lives in a spirit of charity than the consistent omissions of a Government frozen in the ice of its own indifference." And then he went on: "There is a mysterious cycle in human events. To some generations much is given. Of other generations much is expected. This generation of Americans has a rendezvous with destiny." As the crowd roared its approval, he concluded: "I accept the commission you have tendered me. I join with you. I am enlisted for the duration of the war."

During the campaign, he continued to hammer on the same theme. At Madison Square Garden in New York City, at the very end of October, he lashed out even more vocally at shortsighted and selfish members of the business community. In a powerful voice, he proclaimed, "Never before in all our history have these forces been so united against one candidate as they stand today. They are unanimous in their *hate* for *me—and I welcome their hatred*." As the crowd noise swelled, he concluded, gently at first, then increasingly loudly, "I should like to have it said of my first Administration that in it the forces of selfishness and of lust for power met their *match*. I should like to have it said of my second Administration that *in it these forces met their master*."

Roosevelt won in a landslide. He carried every state but Maine and Vermont, gaining the largest popular vote plurality in history, approximately 27.75 million to 16.68 million, and an overwhelming electoral vote margin of 523–8. There were now larger Democratic margins in both the House of Representatives and the Senate. Roosevelt was in an even better position than before.

In winning reelection in 1936, FDR built on Al Smith's earlier efforts to appeal to people in the cities and in so doing put together a new electoral coalition that dominated American politics for nearly 40 years. It included the urban masses, particularly workers from various ethnic groups, and substantial numbers of Jews and Catholics. Of the nation's cities with populations over 100,000, Roosevelt won 104 to Landon's 2. He enjoyed the strong support of labor, thankful for his actions in underscoring the right to organize and bargain collectively. But he also appealed to middle-class homeowners grateful for mortgage assistance and to farmers and other rural voters, many of them from the South, who appreciated the efforts to revive agriculture. African Americans, who had long voted Republican—for the party of Abraham Lincoln, the Great Emancipator—now became part of the Roosevelt coalition, as many blacks benefited from relief programs that provided them, like other poor Americans, with a means of support.

In his second inaugural address, in January 1937, Roosevelt reached out to those Americans still suffering from the ravages of the Depression. "In this nation I see tens of millions of citizens who at this very moment are denied the greater part of what the very lowest standards of today call the necessities of life," he said. "I see one-third of a nation ill-housed, ill-clad, ill-nourished." He was making an implicit promise to those people as he declared, "The test of our progress is not whether we add more to the abundance of those who have much; it is whether we provide enough for those who have too little."

As he promised to help the poor, FDR was particularly concerned about the actions of the Supreme Court. Cases challenging key provisions of the New Deal were working their way through the court system, and federal district judges had issued more than a thousand injunctions keeping the government from carrying out laws passed by Congress. The Supreme Court was the last court of appeal, but Roosevelt could expect no support on that front. Consisting entirely of justices appointed by FDR's predecessors, it took a profoundly conservative view of the Constitution and the legitimate powers of government. Justice Harlan Fiske Stone, one of the more liberal members, later observed that Willis Van Devanter, his archconservative colleague, "conceived it his duty to declare unconstitutional any law which he particularly disliked." Initially, the Court upheld state laws providing a moratorium on mortgage foreclosures and permitting price fixing, and, by a 5–4 vote, it approved a national measure eliminating gold-payment requirements in private contracts. Then, in May 1935, as Justice Owen Roberts joined his more conservative colleagues, it struck down the federal Railway Retirement Act by a 5–4 vote. And in a unanimous decision in May 1935 in the *Schechter* case, it invalidated the NRA with the argument that Congress had overstepped the bounds of the interstate commerce clause and, in what Justice Benjamin Cardozo called "delegation running riot," had gone too far in extending regulatory authority. Roosevelt was furious. Talking to reporters, he called the Court's opinion "a horse-and-buggy definition of interstate commerce."

But the Supreme Court was not finished. In January 1936, by a 6–3 vote in another bombshell ruling in *U.S. v. Butler*, it struck down the processing tax of the AAA, in a decision Justice Stone termed a "tortured construction of the Constitution." In the spring of that year, the Court continued its attack on the government's efforts to deal with the Depression by finding first a national coal conservation act and then a New York state minimum-wage law unconstitutional.

An irate FDR declared that the Supreme Court had created a "'no-man's land' where no Government—State or Federal—could function." It was bad enough to have lost measures aiming to promote industrial and agricultural recovery. But the Court was about to rule soon on two of the New Deal's most important measures that had been passed the year before—the National Labor Relations Act and the Social Security Act. If it overturned those statutes, there would be virtually nothing left.

The president had already been thinking of ways of circumventing the Supreme Court. A constitutional amendment was one possibility, but Roosevelt understood the difficulties of both passage and ratification. Instead, he decided to pursue a potentially easier legislative approach. On February 5, 1937, without any advance warning, he asked Congress for a statute giving him the authority to appoint up to six new Supreme Court justices, one for every justice who failed to retire at the age of 70. He also requested the right to appoint up to 44 new federal judges for the lower courts. Such additions, he argued, were necessary in the interest of efficiency.

The Court-packing plan was a huge mistake. Initially it seemed that with his overwhelming majorities in both houses of Congress, Roosevelt was sure to prevail, but his critics chipped away at the proposal. They pointed out that efficiency was not a pressing concern; they noted that age was not the real issue either, for Justice Louis Brandeis, 81 years old, was part of the Court's more liberal bloc. With regard to the issue of enlarging the Court, there was nothing sacred about the number of sitting Supreme Court justices, which had varied at different times in the Court's history. But this proposed enlargement looked like a transparent political ploy. It was, in the words of the usually sympathetic *New York World-Telegram*, "too clever, too damned clever."

Moreover, Roosevelt seemed to be attacking one of the nation's most important symbols. The notion of an independent judiciary was an important part of America's collective political identity, all the more important in the face of threats to well-being and stability in hard times. Roosevelt's effort to fiddle with it seemed to be all wrong. At the same time, it came just after he had asked Congress for legislation to reorganize the executive office, to give him greater staff support in the interest of good management. Taken together, the two measures opened FDR to the charge that he was seeking to impose a dictatorship on the United States.

Congressional opposition mounted. Because he had kept his intentions hidden, the president had failed to build the necessary consensus for passage of the desired legislation. As Kentucky Senator Alben W. Barkley later noted, Roosevelt was a "poor quarterback. He didn't give us the signals of the play." Nor did he enjoy the support of Vice President John Nance Garner, presiding officer of the Senate, who stood in the lobby of the chamber during the reading of the president's bill with a hand holding his nose in disgust and his thumb pointing down. With a Gallup Poll showing 53 percent opposed to the president's plan, Congress appeared able to hold its ground.

In the end, the Court itself shifted course in the midst of the furor. The justices realized that it was difficult, even wrong, to ignore the overwhelming public sentiment that wanted to give the administration the tools to deal with the economic crisis. At the end of March, in a 5–4 decision, with Justice Roberts rejoining the more liberal bloc, the Court upheld a Washington state minimum wage law, just like the New York statute it had earlier declared unconstitutional. Two weeks later, Roberts again voted with the 5–4 majority that found the Wagner Act—the NLRA—constitutional. Toward the end of May, the Court accepted the unemployment-insurance provisions of Social Security Act, and also upheld old-age pensions. At about the same time, Justice Willis Van Devanter announced his intention of retiring, which meant that FDR would have his first chance to make an appointment to the Court.

Roosevelt got the Court he wanted and needed, but in the process he lost valuable support in Congress. New Deal measures would henceforth be safe from the intrusion of the Supreme Court, which now approved the increased scope of economic regulation, but the fight in Congress, which refused to go along with Roosevelt on the issue of court expansion, helped a conservative coalition coalesce. It had a powerful impact on the rest of Roosevelt's presidency. Republicans and Southern Democrats now worked more closely together and checked the momentum of the New Deal. The heady days of 1933 and 1935, when it had appeared FDR could get anything he wanted, were gone. In 1937, Roosevelt enjoyed limited legislative success. Henry Wallace perhaps overstated the case when he observed that "the whole New Deal really went up in smoke as a result of the Supreme Court fight," but the relationship with Congress had changed.

Meanwhile, Roosevelt faced turbulence on the labor front. In the fall of 1935, the irascible John L. Lewis of the United Mine Workers had demanded that the conservative American Federation of Labor (AFL) organize factory workers into industrial unions. To bring pressure, he had helped create the Committee for Industrial Organization (CIO), which later split entirely from the AFL and renamed itself the Congress of Industrial Organizations. In mid-1936, Lewis decided to take on U.S. Steel and, working with the Steel Workers Organizing Committee, made plans for a major strike. Before it took place, at the very end of the year, automobile employees at the General Motors (GM) plant in Cleveland, Ohio, went on strike first. Two days later, automotive workers at the Fisher Body Plant Number One in Flint, Michigan, embarked on a different kind of strike. Instead of walking out, they simply sat down and refused to leave the factory. GM employees elsewhere followed suit.

The automobile workers had legitimate grievances. Though the hourly wage rate was good, gross income was small, since GM—and the other automobile manufacturers—periodically shut down the assembly line to retool and prepare the machinery for new models. Workers also faced foremen who treated them arbitrarily, firing or penalizing them at will. Conditions became even worse as the Depression dried up the market for new cars.

The sit-down strike at Fisher One cut off much of GM's production by preventing the manufacture of parts used to assemble cars in other factories. For the next six weeks, the strikers remained inside the plant, determined not to leave until GM recognized their union—the United Auto Workers (UAW)—as the legitimate bargaining unit and agreed to a minimum wage and a shorter workweek. Although GM called the strike illegal and tried to blame Communists or other outside agitators, that approach failed to work. The strikers ignored a court injunction ordering them to leave and took over several adjacent plants. Michigan Governor Frank Murphy chose not to mobilize the National Guard to break the strike, recognizing the inevitable bloodshed he would face if he did. Instead, he provided relief payments for the strikers' families.

FDR, meanwhile, quietly urged GM to recognize the union. Always ambivalent about organized labor, he preferred to work behind the scenes to bring about an acceptable result. Governor Murphy, in turn, solicited the help of CIO head Lewis to get the strikers to moderate their demands. After 44 days of the strike, Lewis signed an agreement with GM recognizing the UAW as the bargaining agent of the auto workers. The workers had won a dramatic victory. Acknowledging the result, U.S. Steel quickly certified the Steel Workers Organizing Committee as the legitimate bargaining agent in that industry and so headed off a strike.

Roosevelt was still concerned about recovery. Economic conditions had been improving slowly in the past few years, despite the elimination of the NRA. By the spring of 1937, industrial output levels were finally higher than in 1929, even though employment levels still lagged behind. Then in the summer of 1937, the economy faltered again. Industrial activity plummeted and, by December, The *New York Times* business index had toppled from 110 to 85, wiping out the gains of the past two years. In the fall, the stock market plunged, with the Dow-Jones average dropping from 190 to 115 between August and October. Corporate profits dropped and between Labor Day and the end of the year, two million people lost their jobs. "We are headed right into another Depression," Secretary of the Treasury Morgenthau told the president.

The recession occurred as a direct result of government policy. The slow recovery between 1933 and 1937, particularly in the last two years, had been largely stimulated by major expenditures—a bonus to veterans and the many WPA and PWA projects. In 1936 alone, the New Deal had spent about $4 billion more than it received from taxes, and that spending increased consumption and encouraged economic recovery. In 1937, there were no further bonus payments, and Roosevelt, worried about inflation, slashed WPA and PWA spending. That effort to balance the budget, which operated in the black for the first three quarters of 1937, coupled with a more restrictive monetary policy, brought on the recession.

At first, FDR was relatively sanguine. Despite the troubling economic indicators, he knew that conditions were better than they had been in 1932. Relief programs were helping the unemployed, banks were secure, and farmers were being assisted by benefit payments. People were suffering again, Roosevelt acknowledged, but they showed "more perplexity than fear." As his advisors argued about what to do, he waited to decide what approach to take. In March 1938, Morgenthau told the president, "As I see it, what you are doing now is just treading water . . . to wait to see what happens this spring," to which Roosevelt replied, "Absolutely."

Finally, in mid-April, the president was ready to act. He asked Congress for a large public-works package, and the legislators complied. In June, Congress approved a $3.75 billion measure that provided the PWA with about $1 billion and the WPA with more than $1.4 billion, together with funds for other relief agencies as well. Slowly in the summer of 1938, the economy began to improve. Though Roosevelt proclaimed, "We are again on our way," unemployment levels remained high, with 9 million people still out of work a decade after the stock market crash of 1929.

The recession compromised the continuing efforts of the New Deal. After the dismal legislative record in 1937, Roosevelt enjoyed only modest success in 1938. He managed to secure passage of the Fair Labor Standards Act, prohibiting child labor and mandating a 40 cent minimum hourly wage and a 40-hour work week, though it contained a multitude of exemptions that compromised its effectiveness. He also pushed through a new AAA statute, to replace the earlier measure the Supreme Court had found unconstitutional, making soil conservation efforts permanent and authorizing crop loans and crop insurance. The bill to reorganize the executive branch failed in 1938, and only passed in watered down form the next year.

Frustrated with a recalcitrant Congress, Roosevelt decided to strike out against conservatives in the Democratic Party he regarded as responsible for the stalemate. In the summer of 1938, he traveled around the country, challenging in a number of primary campaigns legislators who had opposed key New Deal measures. But the trip—like the entire effort to purge the party—was ill-advised and unsuccessful. In the midterm elections in November, Republicans gained 81 seats in the House of Representatives and 8 in the Senate.

The New Deal was effectively over. Roosevelt recognized that his broad-based program had run its course. In his annual message to Congress in January 1939, he requested no new economic or social measures, and acknowledged, "We have now passed the period of internal conflict in the launching of our program of social reform. Our full energies may now be released to invigorate the processes of recovery in order to preserve our reforms." Congress, meanwhile, cut back on a number of programs, such as the Federal Theatre Project, slashed other relief appropriations, and challenged some of the president's appointments.

Roosevelt's New Deal never did bring about full-scale economic recovery. The president embarked on a variety of often contradictory initiatives, only seldom following the kind of consistent economic course that might have had a more powerful impact. To be fair, economists were just beginning to understand how to deal effectively with the business cycle in a complex capitalist economy, but even when they spoke out, their voices were seldom heeded.

English economist John Maynard Keynes was in the forefront of the effort to understand how to deal with a major depression. In 1936, he published his seminal book *The General Theory of Employment, Interest and Money*, though he had been lecturing about the ideas to his Cambridge University students even before the work appeared in print. Keynes challenged the accepted wisdom that business cycles were inevitable and that improvement would occur naturally in due course. He argued that depression in the modern world was equilibrium at a low level, and would not disappear without aggressive measures.

Ideally, private business investment could provide the necessary stimulus, and Keynes counseled working with businessmen. "Businessmen have a different sense of delusions from politicians," he once observed, "and need, therefore, different handling. They are, however, much milder than politicians, at the same time allured and terrified by the glare of publicity, easily persuaded to be 'patriots,' perplexed, bemused, indeed terrified, yet only too anxious to take a cheerful view, vain perhaps but very unsure of themselves, pathetically responsive to a kind word. You could do anything you liked with them, if you would treat them (even the big ones) not as wolves and tigers, but as domestic animals by nature, even though they have been badly brought up and not trained as you would wish."

But if businessmen were uncooperative and failed to provide the necessary investment, the government could step in with forceful fiscal policy measures. Pump-priming—a small stimulus to get the system started again—was not sufficient, Keynes declared. Rather, deliberate, sustained, countercyclical spending was required. Such spending could take a variety of different forms. Keynes favored spending for public works, but there were alternatives: "If the Treasury were to fill old bottles with banknotes, bury them at suitable depths in disused coal-mines which are then filled up to the surface with town rubbish, and leave it to private enterprise on well-tried principles of *laissez-faire* to dig the notes up again . . . there need be no more unemployment . . . It would indeed be more sensible to build houses and the like; but if there are political and practical difficulties in the way of this, the above would be better than nothing." An alternative way of putting money into the economy would be by cutting taxes, to increase consumption and thereby to encourage new investment.

At the end of 1933, Keynes wrote an open letter to Roosevelt, published in the *New York Times*. In it, the economist pointed to the "double task, recovery and reform" that faced FDR, but noted that "even wise and necessary reform may, in some respects, impede and complicate recovery. For it will upset the confidence of the business world and weaken its existing motives to action before you have had time to put other motives in their place." Keynes questioned the effectiveness of the NRA, which seemed to him to be a "wrong choice" given its failure to promote new investment and instead put "overwhelming emphasis on the increase of national purchasing power resulting from governmental expenditure . . . Nothing else counts in comparison with this."

Keynes visited Washington, D.C., in June 1934, but his conversation with Roosevelt was unsuccessful. Though FDR wrote to Felix Frankfurter, an adviser who taught at the Harvard Law School, that he had met Keynes and found him a fine fellow, the president also remarked to Frances Perkins after the visit, "I saw your friend Keynes. He left a whole rigaramole of figures. He must be a mathematician rather than a political economist." Keynes, in turn, told Perkins that he had "supposed the President was more literate, economically speaking."

Keynes wrote again to Roosevelt in 1938, and this time Morgenthau, who favored a balanced budget, answered for the president in a noncommittal way. But by that time others in the administration had embraced the basic ideas Keynes espoused. Lauchlin Currie, a staff member at the Federal Reserve Board, was one of those who argued for a Keynesian approach. Marriner Eccles, governor of the Federal Reserve system, believed much the same thing, declaring that "the Government must be the compensatory agent in this economy; it must unbalance its budget during deflation and create surpluses in periods of great business activity," though he claimed he had not heard of Keynes.

The Keynesian analysis helps explain why recovery measures did not work. The NRA sought to raise prices by constricting output, which had the effect of discouraging increased private investment. The PWA had money to spend on public works, but Harold Ickes dispensed it so slowly at the start that it had little effect. The processing tax that was part of the AAA took money out of circulation, as did the Social Security tax, even before the new system began paying out pensions. Both of those measures therefore had precisely the opposite effect from what Keynes counseled. The New Deal never made a firm commitment to the kind of deficit spending Keynes advocated. There were deficits, to be sure, but they came about as a result of relief expenditures rather than as a deliberate effort to revive the economy.

Nor, after his first two years in office, did Roosevelt seek the support of the business community as Keynes suggested. A good number of important New Deal measures alienated business interests. Many businessmen were unhappy with the significant concessions granted to labor, both in Section 7(a) of the NIRA and later in the Wagner Act. They criticized the new Securities Exchange Commission, which started to regulate trading on Wall

Street in 1934, and lashed out at the Public Utilities Holding Company Act of 1935, even watered down, for its intention of eliminating multilayered public power conglomerates not in the public interest. They were angry about New Deal tax measures, such as the Wealth Tax Act of 1935, which sought to make taxation more equitable. They were furious when the New Deal embarked on an antitrust program toward the end of the 1930s. All of those initiatives were important—and Roosevelt may well have been unable to counter business hostility. But, because of the way his programs aroused the resentment of business interests and discouraged new investment, they impeded economic recovery as the Depression dragged on.

Moreover, while Roosevelt's often contradictory initiatives made a difference in people's lives, they overlooked some Americans. African Americans benefited from a number of New Deal programs, like the WPA, which offered relief to the poor regardless of the color of their skin. They found other programs less acceptable. Black sharecroppers were often the ones driven from the land when larger farmers accepted AAA payments to produce less as a way of stabilizing agricultural prices. They were not allowed in all-white model towns built by the TVA, as the government sought to avoid challenging local customs mandating segregation in the South. They complained about discrimination in relief allocations. One black resident of Reidsville, Georgia, grumbled that "the releaf officials here . . . give us black folks, each one, nothing but a few cans of pickle meat and to the white folks they give blankets, bolts of cloth and things like that." Relief payments in Atlanta, for example, reflected discriminatory policies in the implementation of federal programs. While white relief clients received an average of $32.66 per month, blacks got only $19.29.

African Americans were at the same time troubled by Roosevelt's unwillingness to support an antilynching bill. The National Association for the Advancement of Colored People (NAACP) had long advocated such a measure to curb vigilante attacks aimed mostly at blacks. "First things come first," the president said, "and I can't alienate certain votes I need for measures that are more important at the moment by pushing any measures that would entail a fight." He explained his reasoning to Walter White, the first African-American head of the NAACP: "The Southerners by reason of the seniority rule in Congress are chairmen or occupy strategic places on most of the Senate and House committees. If I come out for the anti-lynching bill now, they will block every bill I ask Congress to pass to keep America from collapsing. I just can't take that risk."

Nevertheless, even if they were sometimes disappointed, African Americans appreciated the assistance they did receive and voted for FDR in record numbers. Robert Vann, publisher of the *Pittsburgh Courier*, a black weekly, summed up prevailing sentiment when he advised blacks to "go home and turn Lincoln's picture to the wall. That debt has been paid in full."

They also applauded the efforts of Eleanor Roosevelt, who was much more sympathetic and supportive than her husband. When the Daughters of the American Revolution refused to allow Marian Anderson, a black contralto, to sing at Constitution Hall in Washington, D.C., which they owned, Eleanor publicly resigned from the organization and then worked with Harold Ickes to arrange for the concert to take place at the Lincoln Memorial, where it attracted an audience of 75,000 listeners.

For their part, Native Americans largely appreciated such contributions as the Indian Reorganization Act of 1934, sometimes called the Indian New Deal. It ended the

"Mother Wilfred wrote a bad word!"

Though most Americans supported FDR, some bitterly opposed him and could not even bear to use his name. This cartoon highlights that animosity.

pressure on Indians to assimilate, restored to them control over their land, and helped tribes establish self-government while preserving ancestral traditions. The measure was an effort to reverse the policy of the past century, though some Indians criticized what they called a "back-to-the-blanket" approach that failed to recognize the needs of modern times.

As much as he appealed to millions of Americans, FDR aroused the vitriolic resentment of others. Well-to-do conservatives, in particular, called Roosevelt "a traitor to his class," and some refused to call him by name, referring to him only as "that man." They disliked the regulatory state and feared the centralization of the federal government. Some regarded Roosevelt as a demagogue much like Adolf

Hitler; others, like Republican Senator Robert A. Taft of Ohio, regarded him as a "Red" and declared that the "whole Roosevelt Administration was penetrated by Communists from top to bottom." A cartoon in *Esquire* magazine showed a young boy writing "Roosevelt" on the sidewalk in front of a house while another youngster talked to a woman standing by the front door. The caption read, "Mother, Wilfred Wrote a Bad Word."

That hostility permeated the political process. It gave rise to the increasingly important coalition of Republicans and Southern Democrats, which began to coalesce in the fight over packing the Supreme Court, and which finally brought the New Deal to a halt at the end of the 1930s.

But Roosevelt left a profound mark during the decade of hard times. He had a tremendous resonance with the American people, less evident in his early career but visible in full force in the 1930s. As Senator Elbert Thomas of Utah once observed, FDR "seems to really have caught the spirit of what one of the Hebrew prophets called the desire of the nations," and he was able to translate that spirit into political support for programs he wanted. At the same time, he had a sense of vision that guided his actions. "We are going to make a country in which no one is left out," he once told Frances Perkins, and he made good on his commitment to provide at least a measure of social and economic security to all Americans. In the years that followed his tenure in the White House, the American government was dedicated to helping those who could not help themselves, as the nation moved into the era of the welfare state.

Roosevelt was equally responsible for shaping the modern American presidency. His advisers helped draft legislation and guided it through the legislative process far more aggressively than his predecessors. The numerous alphabet agencies, sometimes working collaboratively, sometimes coming into conflict with one another, reflected the growth of big government in the effort to provide Americans with the help and support they required.

With his resonant voice, so suited to radio, FDR spoke to millions of Americans in their homes and persuaded them that everyone was working together toward a common end. His willingness to talk to the press in a relaxed, bantering way likewise helped keep people informed about what the New Deal was trying to do. There was now a national community, to which most Americans felt they belonged.

For Roosevelt managed to restore a sense of hope and confidence in America itself. In a time of turbulence, he helped democracy survive, in such a way, as columnist Dorothy Thompson observed in 1940, that "our basic institutions are still intact," and he reassured the American people that everything was going to be all right. From the depths of despair, they listened to him, believed him, and supported him. They applauded his experimental approach, his willingness to "take a method and try it," and if it did not work, to try another. And in the course of trying, they finally found some solutions that worked.

Yet the effort took its toll on FDR. When he had run for reelection in 1936, he had seemed relaxed and comfortable. "On none of his predecessors has the office left so few marks as on Mr. Roosevelt," Anne O'Hare McCormick of the *New York Times* reported. "He is a little heavier, a shade grayer; otherwise he looks harder and in better health than on the day of his inauguration. His face is so tanned that his eyes appear lighter, a cool Wedgewood blue; after the four grilling years since the last campaign, they are as keen, curious, friendly and impenetrable as ever." A year later, as FDR faced mounting resistance as a result of the Supreme Court fight and the growth of the conservative coalition in Congress, he looked more tired. "The President is showing the strain," Harold Ickes wrote in his diary. "He looks all of 15 years older since he was inaugurated in 1933. I don't see how anyone could stand the strain he has been under."

The strain continued for the next three years. By 1940, near the end of his second term, with the New Deal basically over, Roosevelt was ready to retire to his home in Hyde Park. Then, however, the increasingly turbulent international scene and the onset of another world war in both Europe and Asia changed the political landscape.

7

The Road to War

For the entire duration of the New Deal, Franklin Roosevelt faced equally serious difficulties on the world stage. The fragile peace hammered out in the Treaty of Versailles at the end of the Great War had begun to erode in the early 1930s as empires in both Europe and Asia sought to expand beyond established borders. On assuming the presidency in 1933, FDR had to deal not only with the debilitating economic depression at home but with the threat to stability around the globe. A little more than a month before his own inauguration, Adolf Hitler became chancellor of Germany, and his efforts to consolidate his power placed the two nations on a collision course. Though Roosevelt had run for vice president in 1920 on an internationalist ticket that endorsed Woodrow Wilson's vision of a League of Nations, as he began his campaign for the presidency a decade later, he rejected that approach. In 1932, well aware of isolationist sentiment in the United States, he issued a public statement opposing American entry into the World Court. But as the decade unfolded, he recognized the growing risk to American interests and sought to educate the American people about overseas conflicts they might not be able to avoid.

The international threats were real. Hitler posed the major menace in the 1930s, but he was not the first to threaten the peace in Europe. Turbulence began in the preceding decade, when Fascist leader Benito Mussolini assumed power in Italy in 1922. His party believed in a strong national government able to quell any socialist uprising, a genuine danger after the Bolshevik victory in the Russian Revolution in 1917 and the Communist commitment to spread the seeds of revolution elsewhere. In Italy, Mussolini established a powerful dictatorship. The Fascist ideology included a commitment to strong, efficient leadership; Mussolini, who came to be called *Il Duce*, made the trains run on time, but at the expense of national liberty and democracy. He also sought to create an empire in the Mediterranean region and in Africa. In the fall of 1935, Italian troops invaded Ethiopia, in East Africa. Mussolini's son boasted that he enjoyed the "magnificent sport" of watching his African victims blow apart like "a budding rose unfolding." Italy conquered Ethiopia the next year.

Germany, too, succumbed to dictatorship. Hitler, head of the National Socialist German Workers' (Nazi) Party, subscribed to the same authoritarian principles as Mussolini. Germany resented the punitive Treaty of Versailles, and the country also suffered from serious inflation spiraling out of control. Imprisoned in 1923 for a failed right-wing attempt to overthrow the government, Hitler wrote an autobiography entitled *Mein Kampf (My Struggle)*, which described his antipathy for Jews and laid out his ultimate goal of acquiring *lebensraum*—living space—in any areas German speakers lived. In a number of elections in the early 1930s, the Nazis became increasingly powerful and, after becoming chancellor, Hitler quickly consolidated his position. On March 5, a day after FDR became president of the United States, Hitler seized absolute power in Germany.

The Nazi dictator moved quickly in his campaign to take control of much of Europe. In 1933, Germany withdrew from a disarmament conference in Geneva, Switzerland, and then from the League of Nations itself. In early 1934, Hitler denounced the disarmament clauses of the Treaty of Versailles and announced Germany's intention of rearming. Two years later, he moved German troops into the Rhineland, a demilitarized area running along Germany's western border. In the fall of 1936, Italy and Germany formed an alliance, known as the Rome-Berlin Axis.

Meanwhile, Asia faced similar disruption. Japan had demonstrated its military strength in its victory over Russia in a war in 1905 and, in the years that followed, it modernized its military machine. Japan had, at the same time, undergone political liberalization in the 1920s, but the problems of the worldwide depression led the military to reassert its power. As leaders of the Army demanded that their island nation expand into what came to be called the Greater East Asia Co-Prosperity Sphere, they strengthened a dictatorial hold over Japan. In September 1931, Japanese and Chinese soldiers fought over a railroad line near Mukden, the capital of Manchuria in China. Japan occupied Mukden, seized towns a hundred miles away and, within a few months, occupied most of Manchuria. The next year Japan established a puppet regime and renamed the country Manchukuo. Meanwhile, in early 1932, the Japanese also attacked Shanghai, in China, but withdrew in response to hostile world opinion. A critical League of Nations resolution led Japan, like Germany, to leave the organization. Several years later, toward the end of 1936, Japan signed an Anti-Comintern Pact with Germany, aimed at stopping Soviet efforts to promote revolution elsewhere. Italy joined the alliance the next year.

The United States, still under the leadership of Herbert Hoover, responded to the Japanese attack in Manchuria with a policy of nonrecognition. Because America had never joined the League of Nations, it could not demand support from the world organization, and so Secretary of State Henry L. Stimson instead presented the Japanese ambassador with a note declaring that the United States would not recognize the legality of any agreement or treaty that impaired American treaty rights or accept any new agreements "which relate to the sovereignty, the independence, or the territorial and administrative integrity of the Republic of China, or to the international policy relative to China, commonly known as the open-door policy." It was a weak and ineffectual response, and one that made little difference, but it was endorsed by the president-elect.

For Roosevelt, like most Americans, had no desire to become involved in any international crisis. He understood the long tradition of isolation, dating to the seventeenth century Puritans who had come to America to escape the strictures of life in Europe and had hoped, in the words of leader John Winthrop, to build a "city upon a hill" to provide an example to the rest of the world. He was aware that the very first president, George Washington, had warned in his farewell address at the end of the eighteenth century against "the insidious wiles of foreign influence," and he recognized as well the pervasive sense of disillusionment after the Great War. The United States had finally plunged into that conflict full of energy and exuberance, and had helped tip the balance in favor of Great Britain and France, yet in the troubling postwar world wondered if the heroic efforts of the doughboys had made any difference. "Rejection of Europe," according to novelist John Dos Passos, "is what America is all about."

Throughout the 1920s and into the 1930s, Roosevelt went out of his way to affirm his antiwar credentials. As the outside world became increasingly turbulent, he knew he had to say something in response to Hitler's rearmament of Germany and Mussolini's invasion of Ethiopia, but he chose his words carefully. In an Armistice Day speech in 1935, he said that "the primary purpose of the United States of America is to avoid being drawn into war." A war could lead "to economic and social collapse more sweeping than any we have experienced in the past." America's role was to stand back and continue to provide a peaceful model for nations at war. As he told William Dodd, the American ambassador to Germany, "I do not know that the United States can save civilization but at least by our example we can make people think and give them the opportunity of saving themselves."

That same general sentiment informed Roosevelt's policy toward Latin America. When an uprising toppled the government of Cuba in 1933, he sent 30 ships to the region to highlight America's presence but refused to countenance military intervention, and, at the end of the year, in what came to be known as the Good Neighbor policy, he renounced the very idea of armed intervention in the affairs of another nation. South Americans hailed him when he visited a number of countries in 1936, though some critics at home were infuriated when he maintained his hands-off approach and refused to respond aggressively to Mexico's expropriation of virtually the entire foreign-owned oil industry in 1938.

Roosevelt used his rhetorical ability to good advantage in a Chautauqua address in the summer of 1936. Affirming, as he had in the past, his commitment to neutrality in the event of another world war, he underscored his dedication to peace on the basis of what he had previously encountered in Europe: "I have seen war. I have seen war on land and sea. I have seen blood running from the wounded. I have seen men coughing out their gassed lungs. I have seen the dead in the mud. I have seen cities destroyed. I have seen two hundred limping, exhausted men come out of line—the survivors of a regiment of one thousand that went forward forty-eight hours before. I have seen children starving. I have seen the agony of mothers and wives. I hate war."

Meanwhile, Roosevelt had to respond to antiwar sentiment in Congress that threatened any latitude for action in the international sphere. In the spring of 1934, Republican Senator Gerald Nye of North Dakota began an investigation of the international armaments industry, which he and others contended had helped cause the last war. The sale of arms, congressional leaders maintained, had undermined disarmament efforts, contributed to the arms race, and extended the war once it began by allowing Germany to continue to fight. By the end of the year, the investigation broadened into an exposé of how economic interests in general had led to American involvement in the Great War. Bankers in the United States, who had loaned large amounts of money to the warring powers, now faced charges that they had been more concerned with profit margin than national interest and had pushed the government to enter the war to protect their own investments. As Nye proclaimed, "When Americans went into the fray, they little thought that they were there and fighting to save the skins of American bankers who had bet too boldly on the outcome of the war and had two billions of dollars of loans to the Allies in jeopardy." Testimony given by financier J. P. Morgan and four members of the influential Du Pont family dramatized the case against the business community. Then the investigating committee went even further and blamed Woodrow Wilson himself for capitulating to the demands of business interests, abandoning his policy of neutrality, and leading the United States into the war.

An idea from Charles Warren, assistant attorney general during the war, added to pressure for congressional action to prevent a recurrence of that pattern. At a

Council on Foreign Relations symposium in early 1934, he suggested that to avoid being drawn into another war, the United States should abandon traditional neutral rights. In an article in the journal *Foreign Affairs* in the spring of 1934, he further proposed that Congress pass legislation prohibiting the export of arms to warring nations, banning loans to such countries, and keeping American citizens from traveling on their ships.

Roosevelt found himself caught in the middle. He knew he could not resist mainstream American sentiment to pass some kind of neutrality legislation. The congressional reaction to a related foreign-policy proposal he made in early 1935 revealed how little latitude he had. Recognizing the need to do something as the international situation deteriorated, he made a belated plea for internationalism by urging the United States to join the World Court. The Court was not likely to be able to do much, but Roosevelt felt it was an important symbol in an increasingly lawless world. The response of the Senate highlighted the strength of isolationist sentiment. Republican Hiram Johnson of California declared, "Once we are in, it does not make any difference whether we are in a little way or whether we are in a long way . . . once we are in, we are in." Democrat Huey Long of Louisiana, always outspoken, raised the specter of intrusion into American affairs in his own colorful—and offensive—way: "We are being rushed pell-mell to get into this World Court so that Señor Ab Jap or some other something from Japan can pass on our controversies." And Thomas Schall, a Republican from Minnesota, was even more vivid as he roared, "To hell with Europe and the rest of those nations."

Though there were 68 Democrats in the Senate, the measure still failed. The vote was 52–36 in favor, as some Democrats abandoned their party, which fell short of the necessary two-thirds majority. A furious Roosevelt wrote,

"As to the thirty-six Senators who placed themselves on record against the principle of a World Court, I am inclined to think that if they ever get to Heaven they will be doing a great deal of apologizing for a very long time—that is if God is against war—and I think He is."

As Congress turned to neutrality legislation in the summer of 1935, Roosevelt sought some room to be able to decide if or how an embargo against warring nations should be applied. Congress refused to comply, with the argument that such flexibility could draw the United States into a future war, just as it had done in the past. Legislators, even Democrats, were determined to tie the president's hands. Nevada Senator Key Pittman told Press Secretary Stephen Early that if FDR persisted in his opposition, he "will be licked as sure as hell." Recognizing the danger to his New Deal initiatives, Roosevelt capitulated, with the request that the neutrality legislation be limited to a period of six months. Congress agreed to that stipulation, and the measure sailed through. Signing it at the end of August, FDR complained that "the inflexible provisions might drag us into war instead of keeping us out," but he was more agreeable to the press as he told reporters that it was "entirely satisfactory."

The Neutrality Act of 1935 required a mandatory embargo of arms to all belligerents once the president proclaimed that a state of war existed. It prohibited American ships from carrying munitions to fighting nations. And it gave the president the power to withhold protection from American citizens on the ships of belligerents, so that they traveled at their own risk.

Five weeks after passage, Roosevelt invoked the new measure. As Italy invaded Ethiopia without a formal declaration of war, FDR was quick to issue a proclamation of neutrality. "They are dropping bombs on Ethiopia—and that is war," he said. "Why wait for Mussolini to say so."

He imposed an arms embargo, warned Americans not to travel on ships of either belligerent power, and told businessmen that they would conduct any trade, even though it was not prohibited, at their own risk. Neither Roosevelt's actions, nor the sanctions imposed by the League of Nations, which the United States had never joined, made much difference as Mussolini completed his conquest.

With the first neutrality measure about to expire in early 1936, Congress debated neutrality policy again. Serious divisions among isolationists complicated the legislative effort. Some members of Congress wanted to cut off all trade in the event of a war; others demanded that neutral rights—allowing for such trade—be upheld. About the only agreement was to reject Roosevelt's request for greater discretion. In the end, the Neutrality Act of 1936 extended the provisions of the prior act for another 14 months, while adding a ban on loans to belligerent governments.

As in the Ethiopian conflict, Roosevelt invoked the neutrality legislation when fighting broke out in Spain in the summer of 1936. As General Francisco Franco headed an army revolt against the Republican government that began in Morocco and then crossed the Mediterranean into Spain, a brutal civil war broke out. The Soviet Union assisted the Republican government; Germany and Italy supported Franco and the Rebels. Great Britain and France argued in favor of nonintervention. Roosevelt followed suit, treating the conflict as if it was not a civil war but a struggle between two foreign nations and imposing an embargo on arms and munitions. He also asked Congress to pass another measure explicitly extending the prior neutrality legislation, drafted originally to deal with a war between different countries, to the Spanish civil war. Congress complied, and, as applied, the joint resolution had the effect of withholding aid to the Republican government, while the Rebels continued to get support from the Nazis and Fascists in Europe. Once again, Roosevelt had domestic issues on his mind—both the forthcoming election and the fight over the Supreme Court—and was unprepared to do anything else in Europe in a conflict most Americans did not care about.

The third and final piece of legislation aimed at insulating the United States from a foreign struggle was the Neutrality Act of 1937. This measure continued the ban on selling arms and loaning money to nations at war and made it illegal for Americans to travel on belligerent vessels. But legislators resisted imposing an embargo on selling other goods to warring countries, out of fear that such a move would cripple the American economy, still suffering from the impact of the Great Depression. Instead, it created a procedure known as "cash and carry." Belligerents could buy nonmilitary goods in the United States, but they had to pay for them immediately—without credit—and transport them in their own vessels and not in American ships.

With passage of that final act, American neutrality policy was firmly in place. Most of the continuing bans were now permanent, while the "cash and carry" provision would expire in mid-1939. In a bitter struggle in Congress, Roosevelt succeeded in getting the House of Representatives, by a close 209–188 vote, to reject a proposed constitutional amendment introduced by Louis Ludlow, a Democrat from Indiana, that would have required a popular referendum before the United States could declare war. That was going too far, Roosevelt argued, observing that the restriction "would cripple any President in his conduct of our foreign relations," while Secretary of State Cordell Hull added that it would "impair disastrously" government efforts to keep the peace. Even without the Ludlow amendment, American policy reflected American sentiment in placing strictures on action in an increasingly turbulent world and in conveying the impression to aggressive nations intent on achieving their own ends that they need not worry about an American response.

Challenges to international peace continued, one after another. In July 1937, Chinese and Japanese troops clashed at the Marco Polo bridge, not far from Peking, and the Japanese then moved on into northern China. A few months later, Mussolini visited Germany, where he addressed 800,000 Germans in Berlin, providing evidence of growing collaboration between Italy and Germany.

Still aware that bold action was impossible, Roosevelt nonetheless decided he needed to speak out. In early October that same year, in a speech in Chicago, a hotbed of isolationist sentiment, he voiced his concerns. He began by declaring that "the present reign of terror and international lawlessness" had "reached a stage where the very foundations of civilization are seriously threatened," and he told listeners that they too were vulnerable. To prevent such an attack, "peace-loving nations must make a concerted effort in opposition to those . . . creating a state of international anarchy and instability from which there is no escape through mere isolation or neutrality." He proposed that this response take the form of a "quarantine" as he continued: "The epidemic of world lawlessness is spreading. When an epidemic of physical disease starts to spread, the community approves and joins in a quarantine of the patients in order to protect the health of the community against the spread of the disease." Then he backed off the bold suggestion by declaring, "America hates war. America hopes for peace. Therefore, America actively engages in the search for peace."

The response was quickly forthcoming. The isolationist press damned the speech. The *Chicago Tribune* declared that Roosevelt had made the city "the center of a world-hurricane of war fright," while the *Wall Street Journal* proclaimed: "Stop Foreign Meddling; America Wants Peace." But other newspapers, such as the the *Washington Post* and the the *New York Times* were more sympathetic. When reporters at a press conference the next day tried to pin FDR down about just what he meant, he was evasive, contending that his comments were consistent with American foreign policy and denying that he sought to undermine the framework of neutrality legislation. "Look," he told reporters, "'sanctions' is a terrible word to use. They are out of the window." That response reflected Roosevelt's own ambivalence and uncertainty about what to do. He may have been groping for a new approach to trouble overseas, but he still was not ready to push too aggressively in a different direction. Even so, he had begun the process of trying to reshape American public opinion. Thanking Endicott Peabody, his old headmaster at Groton, for a telegram of support, Roosevelt wrote, "As you know, I am fighting against a public psychology of long standing—a psychology which comes very close to saying, 'Peace at any price.'" To Joseph Tumulty, Wilson's press secretary several decades earlier, he was similarly critical of the "peace at any price" theory and claimed that he was challenging it now. But the effort was frustrating. "It is a terrible thing," he later said, "to look over your shoulder when you are trying to lead—and to find no one there."

The international situation continued to deteriorate. In November 1937, a month after FDR's Chicago speech, Adolf Hitler told his major advisors what he intended to do next. He wanted to unite all Germans into a new and greater Third Reich. He planned to annex Austria, incorporate the

Sudeten area of Czechoslovakia, which had 3.5 million German speakers, and expand even more widely in search of necessary *lebensraum* in Poland and Ukraine. And, he told them, "Germany's problems could be solved only by means of force." In March 1938, he began to make good on his plans, moving into Vienna and implementing the *Anschluss*—the union—of Germany and Austria, even though such a combination was forbidden by the Treaty of Versailles. The United States acknowledged the aggressive German action by transforming its embassy in Vienna into a lower-level consulate, in recognition of the change in Austria's status.

Czechoslovakia came next. Urged on by Hitler, the Sudeten Germans in the spring of 1938 demanded autonomy from the Czech government, which refused to comply with their request. Czechoslovakia turned to France and Britain, and though France had a diplomatic commitment to aid the Czechs in the event of an attack by another power, France refused to act without British help, and Britain was not ready to challenge Hitler. Neville Chamberlain, prime minister of Great Britain, had already rejected an offer by Roosevelt to hold an international conference of small nations to deal with issues of arms, access to raw materials, and neutral rights that could provide a model for larger nations around the world facing the Fascist threat. Well aware of how unprepared Britain was, Chamberlain had already resolved to follow the path of appeasement.

As the Czech crisis worsened, Hitler demanded the cession of the Sudetenland. Chamberlain traveled to Germany and agreed to Hitler's terms, only to find that Hitler had moved up the date for the transfer of Czech territory. Roosevelt followed what was happening and sent a telegram to all leaders asking for further negotiations to achieve "a peaceful, fair and constructive settlement of the question at issue," and later he proposed a conference of European leaders. Yet at the same time, he told Hitler, "The Government of the United States has no political involvements in Europe and will assume no obligations in the conduct of the present negotiations." At a meeting in Munich, Germany, at the end of September 1938, the Germans got all they wanted, in return for a promise not to seek any further territory. Chamberlain returned to Britain triumphantly proclaiming he had achieved "peace for our time," and Roosevelt, too, was relieved, telling the British leader, "I fully share your hope and belief that there exists today the greatest opportunity in years for the establishment of a new order based on justice and on law." Privately, he compared the British and French diplomats who had accepted the Munich Agreement to Judas Iscariot, but there was little he could do. Three months later, in March 1939, Hitler indicated his contempt for the Munich Agreement by marching into Czechoslovakia and taking it all.

Roosevelt was worried about what was happening to political boundaries in Europe, and he was also concerned with Germany's increasingly aggressive campaign against the Jews. Persecution, foreshadowed in *Mein Kampf*, had begun as soon as the Nazis took power in 1933, and it became more and more intense throughout the decade. The Nuremberg Laws in 1935 restricted Jewish civil rights and barred Jews from certain kinds of employment. After the *Anschluss*, reports reached the United States about new atrocities in Austria. Then, in November 1938, the violence became even more intense. During *Kristallnacht* (Crystal Night), so called because of the pools of broken glass, German hooligans, in a series of government-sanctioned attacks, burned synagogues, destroyed Jewish shops, and looted Jewish homes. It was a clear indication of the enormous threat the Germans posed to Jews on the continent.

Faced with such turbulence, FDR finally accepted the need for revision of the nation's neutrality policy. After the Munich Agreement, the State Department began to consult with congressional leaders about possible changes, and, in his annual message to Congress in early January 1939, Roosevelt obliquely raised the issue of revision. Warning that aggression elsewhere in the world undermined American security, he observed somewhat cryptically that "there are many methods short of war, but stronger and more effective than mere words, of bringing home to aggressor governments the aggregate sentiments of our own people." He then suggested that "our neutrality laws may operate unevenly and unfairly—may actually give aid to an aggressor and deny it to the victim," but he stopped short of making any specific proposals. When Germany invaded Czechoslovakia, Roosevelt said to Senator Tom Connally of Texas, "If Germany invades a country and declares war, we'll be on the side of Hitler by invoking the act," and he told a press conference that revision of neutrality legislation was necessary. But Congress was not ready to act, and months passed with no action.

In August 1939, Germany startled the Western powers once again by signing a nonaggression treaty with the Soviet Union. The Nazi-Soviet Pact, between two nations with very different political systems and a history of antagonism, was an act of expediency providing that each would refrain from attacking the other and would remain neutral in the event of a conflict with other countries.

The Nazi-Soviet Pact allowed Hitler to attack Poland without worrying about resistance from Russia. On September 1, 1939, German troops moved into Poland. William C. Bullitt, American ambassador to France, called Roosevelt before dawn to inform him of the attack. "Mr. President," he said, "several German divisions are deep in

Polish territory. . . . There are reports of bombers over the city of Warsaw." "Well, Bill," FDR responded, "it has come at last. God help us all!" This time, Britain and France honored their commitments and declared war on Germany. World War II had begun.

Two days later, Roosevelt used the radio to deliver another fireside chat to the American people. "Until four-thirty o'clock this morning," he said "I had hoped against hope that some miracle would prevent a devastating war in Europe and bring to an end the invasion of Poland by Germany." He voiced his determination to keep America at peace, but warned that the war was bound to have an impact on the United States. "When peace has been broken anywhere," he declared, "peace of all countries everywhere is in danger." While assuring listeners that "this nation will remain a neutral nation," he refused to follow in the footsteps of Woodrow Wilson, who had called for Americans as individuals to remain neutral in 1914. "I cannot ask that every American remain neutral in thought as well," Roosevelt said. "Even a neutral cannot be asked to close his mind or close his conscience." Two days after the fireside chat, FDR issued a formal declaration of neutrality and invoked the provisions of the 1937 neutrality law.

He then called a special session of Congress to deal with revision of American neutrality policy. He knew it was going to be a tough effort, and he remarked that "I am almost literally walking on eggs," as he asked legislators to return to "the ancient precepts of the law of nations" by repealing the arms embargo. After a strenuous effort to mobilize public opinion and heated debate in Congress, Roosevelt gained the revision he sought and, in early November, signed the Neutrality Act of 1939. It lifted the arms embargo, so that the United States could now sell munitions to Britain and France, provided that they paid cash and carried away their purchases in foreign ships. It was a limited step, but was about all the American public was ready to accept.

At first, the war unfolded rapidly. As Germany strangled Poland into submission in three weeks, the Soviet Union invaded neighboring Finland and, despite fierce Finnish resistance, brought the Nordic nation under control. Though Americans were sympathetic to the Finns for having paid their World War I debt, they simply accepted what FDR privately called the "dreadful rape of Finland." Then followed a six-month stalemate, which Republican Senator William E. Borah of Idaho called the "Phony War," as Hitler consolidated his gains. In early April 1940, Hitler struck again, this time against Denmark and Norway, and the next month against the Netherlands, Belgium, and Luxembourg. Britain managed to evacuate about 338,000 trapped troops from the port of Dunkirk in northern France, but suffered a shattering defeat and lost precious supplies in the process. Soon after the British evacuation, France surrendered to Hitler.

During the Nazi attacks, the British government fell, and Winston Churchill became the new prime minister. In and out of government for the past 40 years, Churchill knew that Britain was reeling and desperately needed help. Eloquently, he asserted his intention of fighting on, even if Hitler invaded his homeland, "until in God's good time, the new world, with all its power and might, steps forth to the rescue and the liberation of the old."

The German blitzkrieg, which culminated in the fall of France, brought a change in American public opinion. Complacency gave way to concern, as a national Committee to Defend America by Aiding the Allies alerted Americans to the very real dangers they faced. Kansas journalist William Allen White, one of the organizers, declared: "As one democracy after another crumbles under the mechanized columns of the dictators, it becomes evident that the future of western civilization is being decided upon the battlefield of Europe. . . . The time has come when the United States should throw its material and moral weight on the side of the nations of western Europe great and small that are struggling in battle for a civilized way of life."

Roosevelt himself played a role in helping shift public opinion. In a speech in June at the University of Virginia in Charlottesville, he declared that it was a "delusion" to think that the United States could exist as "a lone island in a world dominated by the philosophy of force." He went on: "Such an island represents to me and to the overwhelming majority of Americans today a helpless nightmare of a people without freedom—the nightmare of a people lodged in prison, handcuffed, hungry, and fed through the bars from day to day by the contemptuous, unpitying masters of other continents."

Recognizing the need for national unity, Roosevelt brought two prominent Republicans into his cabinet in the spring. Frank Knox, a former Rough Rider in the Spanish-American War of 1898 and Republican vice presidential candidate in 1936, became secretary of the navy. Henry Stimson, who had served as secretary of war under William Howard Taft and then as secretary of state under Hoover, became secretary of war once again. Though an election loomed, FDR wanted to avoid partisan politics as much as he could.

He also listened to Churchill's pleas. Britain desperately needed destroyers to defend itself against an imminent invasion—a threat discovered when cryptographers broke the German military code for messages. At the end of July, Churchill cabled Roosevelt, with whom he was developing an increasingly close relationship, reiterating a request he had made earlier for destroyers to replace those already lost: "Mr. President, with great respect I must tell you that in the long history of the world, this is a thing to do now. . . . I am sure that with your comprehension of the sea affair, you will not let this crux of the battle go wrong for the want of these destroyers."

Roosevelt worked out the arrangements for the transfer of 50 old destroyers in return for eight military bases. International lawyers persuaded the attorney general that the administration could make such a transfer without congressional approval and, in early September, in a message to Congress, the president made the exchange public. Mentioning the destroyers but briefly, he justified the acquisition of the bases stretching from Newfoundland to British Guiana as "an epochal and far-reaching act of preparation for continental defense in the face of grave danger," and he described the transfer as "the most important action in the reinforcement of our national defense that has been taken since the Louisiana Purchase." Churchill was both relieved and delighted to get the ships, declaring that "each destroyer you can spare to us is measured in rubies."

Although America's commitment to neutrality was effectively over, Roosevelt still hedged as he contemplated reelection in 1940. He had been planning to step down after two terms, as all of his predecessors had done, and was already making improvements on his estate in Hyde Park. "I do not want to run," he told his friend Morgenthau, but then went on, "unless between now and the convention things get very, very much worse in Europe." They did, and in the end FDR felt that he had no choice but to remain at the helm. At the Democratic national convention, an orchestrated draft gave him the nomination on the first ballot with Henry A. Wallace his choice as running mate.

In this third campaign for the presidency, Roosevelt faced Wendell Willkie, a corporate lawyer and utilities executive who favored much of what the New Deal had done and was an internationalist in foreign affairs as well. In a speech to the Teamsters Union in September, FDR focused largely on domestic issues, but then told his audience, "I hate war, now more than ever. I have one supreme determination—to do all that I can to keep war away from these shores for all time." A month later, however, in a Columbus Day speech in Dayton, Ohio, he promised to continue supporting Great Britain: "No combination of dictator countries of Europe and Asia will stop the help we are giving to almost the last free people now fighting to hold them at bay." When Congress passed a measure authorizing America's first peacetime draft, he signed it for he recognized the need to bolster military strength, even while worrying about the political consequences.

When Willkie's campaign bogged down and he began to attack the administration's foreign policy, alleging that if Roosevelt won reelection, "you may expect we will be at war," FDR struck back. In Boston, at the very end of October, he proclaimed vigorously, "I have said this before, but I shall say it again and again: Your boys are not going to be sent into any foreign wars." When it was suggested that he might not be able to keep his promise if the nation was attacked, he replied, "If somebody attacks us, then it isn't a foreign war, is it?" Willkie was furious. "That hypocritical son of a bitch!" he declared when he heard about Roosevelt's speech. "This is going to beat me!"

It did. Roosevelt gained 55 percent of the popular vote and won by a margin of 334–197 in the Electoral College. His 5 million vote margin was considerably smaller than his 11 million vote plurality in 1936, and was his narrowest yet, but was still large enough to provide him with a clear-cut victory as he continued to deal with the war.

As the military situation in Europe deteriorated, the United States became more and more involved. Perhaps the most serious problem was that Britain, once a proud imperial power, was running out of money. As Lord Lothian, British ambassador to the United States, told reporters as he returned from a trip for consultations at home, "Well, boys, Britain's broke. It's your money we want." At a meeting of top advisers in Stimson's home a month after the election to talk about financial requirements, Knox asked, "We are going to pay for the war from now on, are we?" Secretary of the Treasury Morgenthau followed up with a question of his own: "Well, what are we going to do, are we going to let them place more orders or not?" A consensus soon emerged as Knox spoke for the group in saying, "Got to. No choice about it."

A few days later, while FDR was sailing on the *U.S.S. Tuscaloosa* in the Caribbean, a Navy seaplane delivered a long letter from Churchill. In it, the British prime minister acknowledged that in another several months, British financial reserves would be gone. "The moment approaches," he said, "when we shall no longer be able to pay cash for shipping and other supplies."

Roosevelt responded in a press conference in mid-December. He began by declaring that America's defense depended on Britain's ability to protect itself. Noting the financial discussions that had been taking place, he proposed a new alternative. He wanted to "get rid of the silly, foolish old dollar sign." He illustrated what he meant with a parable about lending a garden hose to a neighbor whose house was on fire. You lent the hose immediately, he said, without dickering over price and, when the fire was finally out, the neighbor would return the hose. In the same way, the United States would give Britain whatever supplies were necessary, "with the understanding that when the show was over, we would get repaid something in kind, thereby leaving out the dollar mark in the form of a dollar debt and substituting for it a gentleman's obligation to repay in kind." That was the genesis of what came to be called Lend-Lease.

Roosevelt continued his campaign to gain both public and congressional approval for his effort to help Britain. Less than two weeks later, at the very end of December, he addressed the American public in another fireside chat. He warned even more ominously than before about the consequences of an Axis victory for the United States, telling listeners that to avoid conquest, "we must have more ships, more guns, more planes—more of everything. . . . We must be the great arsenal of democracy."

When Congress received the Lend-Lease bill in early 1941, a heated debate followed. Republican Senator Robert A. Taft, of Ohio, said that "lending war equipment is a good deal like lending chewing gum. You don't want it back." Burton Wheeler, Taft's Democratic colleague from Montana, compared Lend-Lease with the AAA policy of plowing up already planted fields in 1933. Lend-Lease was "the New Deal's triple-A foreign policy; it will plough under every fourth American boy." Roosevelt was irate, and called the comment "the rottenest thing that has been said in public life in my generation." Despite isolationist criticism, Congress passed the bill. Roosevelt signed it into law in March and appointed Harry Hopkins to head the agency in charge of sending supplies. That was, the *New York Times* declared, "the day when the United States ended the great retreat which began with the Senate rejection of the Treaty of Versailles and the League of Nations." As *Newsweek* noted earlier, it gave FDR permission to lend "anything from a trench shovel to a battleship."

Meanwhile, with Roosevelt's approval, American military leaders began planning joint strategy with their British counterparts for use if the United States entered the war. Such coordination indicated that the United States, in the words of playwright and speechwriter Robert Sherwood, had entered into a "common law alliance" with Britain.

The United States began to tangle with the Germans. One major problem was increasing German submarine attacks on merchant shipping. Opponents of Lend-Lease had warned against the use of American convoys, but in April, aware that Britain did not have enough escort vessels, FDR made the decision to move beyond the 300-mile neutrality belt the United States was already patrolling and to protect ships to a point midway across the Atlantic. At about the same time, he also made a decision that the United States should occupy Greenland. Protection of Iceland came next. The *U.S.S. Greer*, an American destroyer that had been helping a British patrol plane trail an enemy submarine, was attacked by the vessel; Roosevelt responded by calling German submarines "rattlesnakes of the Atlantic" and implied, without saying so explicitly, that American ships would shoot the submarines on sight. Without a formal declaration, the United States was effectively at war.

As the conflict in Europe unfolded, Japan became increasingly aggressive in Asia. The Japanese campaign to conquer China bogged down, but the success of the Axis powers in the first stages of the war in Europe led Japan to consider moving into Indochina, Malaya, and the Dutch East Indies (now Indonesia). Southeast Asia had necessary supplies of oil and other materials, and Japanese leaders saw their chance to establish what they called the Greater East Asia Co-Prosperity Sphere. As militarists gained control of the Japanese government, in September 1940 Japan signed the Tripartite Pact, a formal alliance with Germany and Italy. The pact recognized German and Italian supremacy in Europe and Japanese supremacy in

East Asia; by its terms the three nations pledged support to one another if attacked by another foe.

Meanwhile, Japan began the process of expansion by pressing for concessions in the Dutch East Indies and Indochina. Well aware the United States was not ready for a war in the Pacific, Roosevelt nonetheless recognized the need to respond. In July 1940, the United States imposed an embargo on export of aviation fuel and the highest grade of scrap iron and steel to Japan. Significantly, the embargo did not include other petroleum products from the United States, so necessary to a Japanese economy dependent on importing 88 percent of its oil. Refusing to be deterred, Japan responded by taking control of all of Indochina in July 1941. Roosevelt, with the approval of his top advisers, froze Japan's assets in the United States and extended the embargo, this time cutting off oil exports as well. "The noose is around Japan's neck at last," declared an editorial in the newspaper *PM*. "For a time it may bluster and retaliate, but in the end it can only whimper and capitulate." Though the American move was intended to pressure the Japanese into halting their advance, it only strengthened their resolve to gain control of oil fields in the Dutch East Indies and of other East Asian areas rich in natural resources.

The United States and Japan were on a collision course. In the summer of 1941, Japanese Prime Minister Fumimaro Konoye proposed a personal meeting with President Roosevelt to try to find a peaceful solution to their problems. Secretary of State Hull rejected the possibility of such a meeting unless Japan first abandoned its aggression in the Far East. With top-level talks impossible, Japan decided to invade the Dutch East Indies before the end of the year. A new prime minister, General Hideki Tojo, was not eager for war, but recognized its likelihood and agreed to set a deadline of midnight on November 30 for the resumption of American trade. If it was not met, Japan would go to war. "Rather than await extinction," he later wrote, "it were better to face death by breaking through the encircling ring and find a way for existence."

Talks with two Japanese envoys continued throughout November, but led nowhere. Although cryptographers had broken the Japanese code, and American diplomats were aware of Japan's aggressive intentions, the charade continued. Messages went back and forth, even as the United States knew that Japan had made a decision to sever diplomatic relations and move toward war, even if it was not sure where an attack might come.

It came on December 7, 1941, and targeted the American Pacific fleet at Pearl Harbor, on the island of Oahu in Hawaii. It destroyed or disabled 19 ships, including 5 battleships, and 150 planes and killed nearly 2,400 servicemen. At home it created first shock, then rage.

The next day, Roosevelt went to Congress. In a short message, angry and eloquent, heard by some 60 million Americans, he called December 7 "a date which will live in infamy" and asked Congress to declare "that since the unprovoked and dastardly attack . . . a state of war has existed." With but a single dissenting vote, Congress complied. Three days later, Germany declared war on the United States. Now the nation was fully involved in the worldwide conflict.

Roosevelt's closest advisers were relieved. Harry Hopkins recorded the sense of a meeting FDR called on December 7: "The conference met in not too tense an atmosphere because I think that all of us believed that in the last analysis the enemy was Hitler and that he could never be defeated without force of arms; that sooner or later we were bound to be in the war and that Japan had given us an opportunity." Henry Stimson felt much the same way: "My first feeling was of relief that the indecision was over and that a crisis had come in a way which would unite all our people."

Roosevelt too was relieved that the waiting was over. For him, as Hopkins noted, it took the question of war or peace "entirely out of his hands, because the Japanese had made the decision for him." He had understood earlier than most Americans that war was going to be unavoidable. Slowly but surely he had helped shape American opinion to support the measures he felt were necessary. Now it was possible to make the full-scale effort to counter the deadly threats to world peace. The task ahead was overwhelming, but Roosevelt was ready. As Eleanor noted later, "In spite of his anxiety, Franklin was in a way more serene than he had appeared in a long time."

8

Commander-in-Chief

Franklin Roosevelt recognized that World War II was the greatest military struggle of all time. World War I, as the Great War now came to be called, had exacted tremendous losses, particularly in the relentless trench warfare that slaughtered millions on both sides, but now new weapons and new machines made the means of destruction even more devastating than before. Bombing from the air with conventional explosives killed soldiers and civilians alike, and the atomic bomb, developed during the war and eventually used on Japan, made it possible to wipe out tens of thousands of people in a single attack. Wartime leaders had even greater responsibility than in the past for making the appropriate decisions to win the war. Close coordination of strategy was necessary to defeat the Germans, Italians, and Japanese, and the Grand Alliance that brought the United States, Great Britain, and the Soviet Union together was the means to that end. But coalitions can be difficult to keep intact, for each nation has its own military aims and strategic priorities, and the three leaders—Roosevelt, Churchill, and Soviet head Josef Stalin—discovered the truth in Churchill's comment that the only thing worse than fighting with allies was fighting without them.

Roosevelt was ready to focus all his attention on the war even before America's formal entrance into the conflict. In a press conference at the end of 1943, he summed up the shift that had occurred with one of the stories he was fond of telling. The New Deal had come about, he said, when the patient—the United States—was suffering from a grave internal malady. But then in the Japanese attack on Pearl Harbor, the patient was in a terrible crash. "Old Dr. New Deal," the president declared, "didn't know 'nothing' about arms and legs. He knew a great deal about internal medicine, but nothing about surgery. So he got his partner, Dr. Win-the-War, who was an orthopedic surgeon, to take care of this fellow who had been in this bad accident." The New Deal was effectively over, Roosevelt acknowledged, and he was ready to subordinate everything to the war effort. FDR, who had loved the sea ever since he was a small boy and had later served nearly eight years as assistant secretary of the navy, enjoyed his role as commander-in-chief. Once at a cabinet dinner, when Secretary of State Hull was about to propose a toast, Roosevelt asked to be addressed as commander-in-chief, and not as president. In his capacity as head of the military, he spent considerable time with army and navy leaders poring over maps and plotting American strategy. He was confident of his capacity to keep track of a dozen details at the same time, and was equally sure of his ability to deal with the other leaders of the Grand Alliance.

Winston Churchill, his counterpart in Great Britain, was an influential leader. The son of an English father and an American mother, he was naturally sympathetic to the United States. A descendent of the First Duke of Marlborough, a general in the late seventeenth and eighteenth centuries, he had played an important part in British politics and public affairs for the past four decades. He had held various cabinet posts, including service as first lord of the admiralty, and he shared FDR's interest in military strategy. Churchill had been out of power in the

1930s because of his opposition to a government plan to move toward implementing limited self-government in the British colony of India and, later, because of his disagreement with Britain's policy of appeasement. Now he was back in office, this time at the top.

Churchill used his rhetorical skills to mobilize his battered followers. He was able to turn a phrase elegantly, as when he acknowledged the contribution of English airmen in the Battle of Britain by saying, "Never in the field of human conflict was so much owed by so many to so few." And he could use repetition with a soaring expressiveness in moving toward a conclusion. Speaking to the House of Commons in mid-1940, he declared: "We shall go on to the end, we shall fight in France, we shall fight on the seas and oceans, we shall fight with growing confidence and growing strength in the air, we shall defend our island, whatever the cost may be, we shall fight on the beaches, we shall fight on the landing grounds, we shall fight in the fields and in the streets, we shall fight in the hills; we shall never surrender."

Churchill's first major task was enlisting the aid of the United States. To that end, he cultivated what became a very special relationship with FDR. The two men had first met in 1918, but had not been in close contact again until 1939, when Churchill joined the British cabinet at the Admiralty and Roosevelt wrote to him, "It is because you and I occupied similar positions in the World War that I want you to know how glad I am that you are back in the Admiralty. . . . What I want you and the Prime Minister to know is that I shall at all times welcome it if you will keep me in touch personally with anything you want me to know about." After he became head of the government, Churchill took to calling himself Former Naval Person in his letters to FDR, to underscore the bond that was growing between them. During the course of the war, the two men corresponded and met regularly, and their friendship helped keep the coalition intact.

The third leader of the Grand Alliance was Stalin. After his early victories in the war, Hitler reneged on the Nazi-Soviet Pact, which he had always viewed as an expedient to buy time and, in June 1941, invaded the Soviet Union. The British and the Russians now found themselves fighting on the same side, and Roosevelt extended limited Lend-Lease assistance to the Soviets even before the United States entered the war.

Stalin was a ruthless dictator. Born in Georgia, in the Caucasus Mountains, he had studied in a seminary before becoming a convert to revolutionary socialism. After the death in 1924 of Vladimir Lenin, the father of the Russian Revolution, Stalin became embroiled in a power struggle from which he emerged supreme. Intent on consolidating Communism in his own country, he nationalized industry and established a collectivized system in agriculture in a series of Five Year Plans, which never worked as well as expected. When he faced opposition in the 1930s, Stalin purged his enemies brutally, either arresting and executing them, or sending them to work camps in Siberia. Estimates of the death toll vary, but millions lost their lives.

Churchill had a long history of antipathy toward Soviet socialism. "No one has been a more consistent opponent of Communism than I have for the last twenty-five years," he acknowledged as the Russians resisted the German attack. "I will unsay no word that I have spoken about it." But given their common enemy, he was prepared to work together with the Communists.

Roosevelt was equally suspicious of the Soviet state. He had moved to extend formal diplomatic recognition to the Soviet Union when he assumed office in 1933, recognizing the futility of the policy of nonrecognition that had prevailed ever since the Bolshevik triumph in the Russian

Revolution of 1917, but he was still wary of Soviet leadership. To the left-leaning American Youth Congress, prior to the attack on Pearl Harbor, he declared, "The Soviet Union, as everybody who has the courage to face the fact knows, is run by a dictatorship as absolute as any other dictatorship in the world." Other American officials shared that view. Army Chief of Staff George C. Marshall called Stalin "a rough SOB who made his way by murder."

Once the Soviet Union joined the Grand Alliance, however, and Stalin played down rhetoric about the inevitable triumph of Communism and highlighted the war as a nationalistic struggle instead, Roosevelt, like Churchill, was realistic about the need to work with the Russians. "I can't take communism," he once said, "but to cross this bridge I would hold hands with the Devil." FDR went out of his way to conciliate Stalin, and to try to establish a personal relationship with him as well, even if it sometimes seemed to be at Churchill's expense. Stalin usually listened quietly, but still felt left out. In mid-1943, he wrote to Roosevelt: "To date it has been like this, the U.S.A. and Britain reach agreement between themselves while the U.S.S.R. is informed of the agreement between the two Powers as a third party looking passively on. I must say that this situation cannot be tolerated any longer."

The Grand Alliance—like any coalition—also had occasional difficulties because each of the major powers had its own war aims. All wanted to defeat Nazism and Fascism and destroy the dictators, to be sure, but after that they had their own national priorities. For Roosevelt, that meant helping shape the American vision of democracy for the postwar world. In a message to Congress in early 1941, even before the attack on Pearl Harbor, he spoke of the "four essential human freedoms"—freedom of speech and expression, freedom of worship, freedom from want, and freedom from fear. Those provided the ideological framework for American views about the meaning of the war. In August of that same year, Roosevelt and Churchill met together off the coast of Newfoundland on the British battleship *Prince of Wales* and, at the end of their conference, issued a joint declaration. Idealistically, the Atlantic Charter opposed "territorial changes that do not accord with the freely expressed wishes of the peoples concerned" and promised to have "sovereign rights and self-government restored to those who have been forcibly deprived of them." For much of the war, Roosevelt also contemplated a postwar peace maintained by "Four Policemen"—the United States, Great Britain, the Soviet Union, and China, which he insisted on regarding as a great power.

Churchill, desperate for a victory that would maintain British survival, thought more in terms of a balance of power. In the postwar world, he wanted to see Western Europe revived and rehabilitated to serve as a buttress against the Soviet Union, which he felt still posed a threat to democracy. Though he was willing to move toward increased self-government for colonial peoples, he was unwilling to go as far as Roosevelt, and he told Parliament that the Atlantic Charter applied to the enemy and not to the British colonies of India and Burma. He had not "become the King's first minister in order to preside over the liquidation of the British Empire," he declared late in 1942.

Stalin, like Churchill, was fighting for the very existence of his nation. Specifically, he wanted recognition of the Soviet need for security in Eastern Europe, which twice in the past 30 years had been the path of a German invasion of Russia, and he was intent on having governments friendly to the Soviet Union in that region. The Soviet Union was willing to adhere to the Atlantic Charter with the qualification that "the practical application of these principles will necessarily adapt itself to the circumstances, needs, and historic peculiarities of particular countries."

The Allies also disagreed over strategy. Soon after the American entrance into the war, Churchill was Roosevelt's guest at the White House, where they reviewed war plans together. Concerned that the United States might be preoccupied with the war in the Pacific, particularly after the devastating Pearl Harbor attack, he pushed for a continued commitment to the "Europe first" approach to the fighting. In their very first conversation at that meeting, Roosevelt reassured Churchill of his agreement with that plan. "The discussion," the prime minister subsequently told his War Cabinet, "was not *whether* but *how*" to implement the strategic focus on the Atlantic. The United States would grapple with Japan in the Pacific on its own, but it would fight together with Great Britain and the Soviet Union in Europe until the war there was won. Roosevelt and Churchill also agreed on a unified Anglo-American military command to coordinate strategic policy. But initially they differed over what that strategy should be.

Roosevelt and his American military advisers—including Secretary of War Stimson and General Marshall—favored an invasion of Europe across the English Channel, followed by a drive toward Germany. Dwight D. Eisenhower, who later came to command all Allied forces in Western Europe, agreed, declaring, "We had to attack to win." Those military leaders wanted to strike at the enemy directly and to defeat Hitler and Mussolini as quickly as possible. Stalin favored the same approach. The Soviet Union was desperate to have the Allies open a second front in Western Europe to take pressure off the war it was waging single-handedly against Germany in Eastern Europe.

In April 1942, Roosevelt sent Marshall and Harry Hopkins, always ready to do what the president asked, to

Britain to persuade Churchill to go along. "Dear Winston," he wrote the prime minister, "What Harry and Geo. Marshall will tell you all about has my heart and *mind* in it. Your people and mine demand the establishment of a front to draw off pressure on the Russians, and those peoples are wise enough to see that the Russians are killing more Germans and destroying more equipment than you and I put together."

But Churchill was reluctant to strike directly too soon. He recalled the devastating trench warfare of World War I, which had wiped out an entire generation of future British leaders, and was unwilling to launch a similar attack until the Allies were sure to win. He also understood that German submarines had sunk so many ships in the Atlantic that the Allies lacked the necessary resources for a massive direct strike. He and the British commanders favored a policy of "tightening the ring" by attacking the Axis powers along the periphery, with initial blows at what he called the "soft under-belly," first in North Africa and then in Italy. Churchill persuaded Roosevelt to abandon plans for a cross-channel invasion in 1942, and secured his agreement for a Mediterranean strategy instead. Roosevelt acquiesced because he recognized the need for further preparation before invading France and understood that an early offensive anywhere could help bolster American confidence at home and in the field and show the Germans a first display of American might. As Marshall, who finally accepted this strategic initiative, noted, "The President considered it very important to morale, to give the country a feeling they are in the war, to give the Germans the reverse effect, to have American troops somewhere in active fighting over the Atlantic."

Whatever the military and political reasoning, Stalin was irate when he learned of the decision. Desperate for a cross-channel invasion to relieve pressure as the Soviet

Union was struggling for survival in a fight with the Axis in Eastern Europe, he viewed any side incursions as unacceptable. "Taking fully into account the present position on the Soviet-German front," he declared, "I must state in the most emphatic manner that the Soviet Government cannot acquiesce in the postponement of a second front in Europe until 1943." As Churchill sought to reassure his Russian ally, Roosevelt counseled, "Your reply to Stalin must be handled with great care. We have always got to bear in mind the personality of our ally and the very difficult and dangerous situation that confronts him. No one can be expected to approach the war from a world point of view whose country has been invaded. I think we should try to put ourselves in his place."

While Roosevelt and Churchill plotted strategy to counterattack in North Africa, the Allies could not avoid the Battle of the Atlantic as the Germans sank 1,664 ships in 1942 alone and continued to hold the upper hand in early 1943. Though Allied ships traveled in convoys, they were still easy prey for the Nazi wolf packs, groups of submarines traveling together. Only the massive American productive effort saved the day, building ships faster than German submarines could destroy them. Planes, too, made the Atlantic sea lanes safer, and new radar systems helped locate enemy ships. Improvements in sonar— sound navigation and ranging—likewise helped detect submerged vessels, which could then be hit when they had to surface. By the middle of 1943, the Navy had seized the initiative, as the Allies regained control of the Atlantic.

Once Roosevelt and Churchill decided where to strike on the offense, military strategists planned the North African invasion. Throughout the summer and the fall of 1942, Roosevelt was impatient for the attack to begin. Worried about both the home front and the Soviet pressure for aggressive action, he wanted the invasion to come, he told Churchill, "at the earliest possible moment. Time is of the essence." Operation TORCH finally got underway on November 8, 1942, as about 90,000 Allied troops, most of them Americans under Eisenhower's command, landed at a series of coastal points in Morocco and Algeria. There they encountered resistance, particularly from the French collaborators who administered the area for the Germans after the fall of France. Now American leaders faced a dilemma: Was there a French commander they could work with, who would be able to persuade the French in North Africa not to fight back? Charles DeGaulle, leader of the Free French resistance, was out of power and difficult to work with. General Henri Giraud, who had been sympathetic to the Vichy French collaborators, was a possibility, but his insistence on taking over command ruled him out. In the end, hoping for a bloodless takeover that avoided killing French soldiers, Eisenhower signed an agreement with Admiral Jean François Darlan, commander-in-chief of the French Armed Forces, who happened to be in North Africa to visit his sick son. He agreed to order a ceasefire, in return for being recognized as having "responsibility for French interests in Africa." Darlan fulfilled his part of the bargain, and the military effort unfolded more easily, but there was an uproar at home. Critics in both Britain and the United States charged that the Allies had failed to confront the enemy head-on and, by making an agreement with notorious collaborators, had sacrificed principle to military expediency. Robert Sherwood, one of FDR's advisers and speechwriters, later noted that to people everywhere, the deal with Darlan "seemed to confirm the impression that, while Americans talked big about the principles of the Four Freedoms and the Atlantic Charter, they actually knew nothing about Europe and could be hoodwinked by any treacherous gangster who offered them collaboration." Tension remained high until Darlan was assassinated on Christmas eve.

Roosevelt and Churchill decided to meet in early January in Casablanca, in Morocco, to plan the next steps in the war. Roosevelt took Harry Hopkins and the American chiefs of staff with him, but deliberately excluded Secretary of State Cordell Hull as, in a pattern that persisted throughout the war, he kept control of diplomacy in his own hands. Buoyant after the first recovery of Axis-held territory, the two heads of state looked ahead to gaining control of all of Africa and to moving into Europe. They decided that Sicily would be the next step. Marshall was irritated at the decision, as he feared that the Mediterranean was becoming a "suction pump," draining resources that could better be used elsewhere. Stalin, who remained vulnerable in Eastern Europe, was even angrier. This was still not the second front that the Soviet Union wanted, and he was upset that it now looked as though a cross-channel invasion could not commence before 1944. An incursion into Sicily, he wrote to Roosevelt, "can by no means replace a Second Front in France."

In the face of Stalin's anger, Roosevelt made an important pronouncement. To persuade the Soviet Union that the Allies were committed to fight until the final defeat of the Axis, he decided to announce the demand of unconditional surrender at Casablanca. He and Churchill talked about it briefly and then, on the last day, Roosevelt spoke out publicly at a press conference. "Peace can come to the world only by the total elimination of German and Japanese war power," he said. "The elimination of German, Japanese, and Italian war power means the unconditional surrender by Germany, Italy, and Japan. . . . It does not mean the destruction of the population of Germany, Italy, or Japan, but it does mean the destruction of the philosophies in those countries which are based on conquest and the subjugation of other people." Although he had almost certainly considered his statement carefully, he tried to make it appear casual and spontaneous so that it did not seem part of a calculated plan to appease Stalin. With his effort to underscore his unwillingness to destroy enemy peoples, he hoped to remind listeners of Ulysses S. Grant's magnanimous gesture in letting Southerners keep their side arms and horses after Robert E. Lee's surrender ended the American Civil War. It was all he could do to reassure Stalin that the Grand Alliance intended to see the war through to the end.

The Italian campaign came next. With Eisenhower again at the helm, it began in Sicily in July and continued on to the Italian mainland in the summer. That next step again came at Churchill's instigation, and while Roosevelt agreed, he did so only on the condition that the attack on Italy use solely "the resources already available," for everything else needed to be stockpiled in Great Britain in preparation for the cross-channel invasion now scheduled for May 1944. Roosevelt was finally becoming impatient with Churchill's peripheral strategy and was willing to listen more closely to his own military advisers, particularly to Admiral William D. Leahy, his own personal chief of staff and chairman of the Joint Chiefs of Staff, who was eager for a direct attack.

The Allied leaders faced political problems in Italy like those they had encountered in North Africa. As the assault on Sicily unfolded, Mussolini finally recognized that he could not counter the Allied attack and resigned. In his place, King Victor Emmanuel III appointed as prime minister Marshal Pietro Badoglio, former chief of the general staff, who was notorious for his brutal role in the Ethiopian campaign. Badoglio quickly entered into secret conversations aimed at bringing about a surrender. American propagandists furiously charged that "Fascism is still in power in Italy," and condemned the "moronic little king" for orchestrating "a political minuet and not the revolution we have been waiting for."

Roosevelt recognized Stalin's growing impatience. The Soviet Union was excluded from participation in the Italian campaign, and the long-sought cross-channel invasion was still a long way off. In May 1943, in a personal message to the Soviet leader, FDR proposed "an informal and completely simple visit for a few days between you and me." He would bring Harry Hopkins, whom Stalin had already met, but not Churchill, in an effort to reach "a meeting of the minds." When Churchill heard about this overture, he was worried, despite Roosevelt's specious disclaimer that the meeting had been "Uncle Joe's" idea. In the end, the three leaders agreed they should all meet in December, in Teheran, the capital of Iran.

That conference took place at the end of November 1943. Accepting an invitation to stay in the Soviet compound, Roosevelt got to meet Stalin in person for the first time, spoke alone with him on several occasions, and worked together with both Stalin and Churchill to plan the final confrontation with the Axis. Roosevelt and Stalin together insisted that OVERLORD, the cross-channel invasion, not be delayed any longer. As Stalin demanded to know a specific date, Roosevelt made a firm commitment to May 1, 1944, and declared, as Churchill looked on, that nothing could change that date. "There was no God-damn alternative left," Hopkins said later in relief. As the meeting went on, Russia reaffirmed its intention of joining the war against Japan once the war in Europe was won. And the three leaders began to plan for the future of Germany. Stalin favored dismemberment, and Roosevelt agreed, over Churchill's objections, but final plans were postponed.

As the conference came to an end, Roosevelt found Stalin serious and grim. Eager to break through this stiffness,

FDR began to banter with Churchill "about his Britishness, about John Bull, about his cigars, about his habits. . . . Winston got red and scowled, and the more he did so, the more Stalin smiled. Finally, Stalin broke into a deep, heavy guffaw, and for the first time in three days I saw light," the president later confided to Frances Perkins. "I kept it up until Stalin was laughing with me, and it was then that I called him 'Uncle Joe.'" And so "the ice was broken and we talked like men and brothers."

While the United States and Great Britain fought with the Germans and Italians in the Atlantic and Mediterranean theaters, the Soviet Union grappled with the German military machine by itself on the eastern front. In the process, it sustained tremendous casualties in what at first appeared to be a hopeless cause. Then, in the monumental Battle of Stalingrad, which lasted from mid-November 1942 until early February 1943, the Soviets defeated the Germans and reached a turning point in the war. With morale boosted, they now pushed the Germans back, but faced fierce resistance in the process. Even so, the Red Army moved relentlessly westward, driving the Germans out of strongholds in eastern Europe, and moving inexorably toward Germany itself.

Meanwhile, the British and Americans embarked on a massive bombing campaign aimed at weakening Germany. Roosevelt had long believed in the importance of air power, remarking even before the conflict began that "pounding away at Germany from the air" could erode German morale. "This kind of war," he argued, "would cost less money, would mean comparatively few casualties, and would be more likely to succeed than a traditional war by land and sea." At first Churchill and the British favored large-scale bombing of cities in an effort to break morale, while Roosevelt and the Americans preferred precision bombing aimed at specific military and industrial targets.

Eventually, the British approach prevailed. But the bombing campaigns were hardly as easy as FDR had anticipated. Accidents claimed some lives, and enemy fire brought numerous airplanes down. Nevertheless, while the bombing failed to break Germany, it did weaken the military machine as the cross-channel invasion approached.

At the same time, Roosevelt faced the crucial question of who would lead the OVERLORD invasion across the English Channel. George Marshall, chairman of the Combined Chiefs of Staff, was the obvious candidate. A man of both intelligence and integrity who almost single-handedly kept the war effort on track, he was the choice of FDR, who knew that Marshall deserved this chance for supreme leadership. "That is one of the reasons I want George to have the big command—he is entitled to his place in history as a great General," Roosevelt told Eisenhower. Both Hopkins and Stimson agreed. Military advisers, on the other hand, told the president that Marshall was essential to keep peace among agencies, services, and allies. In the end Roosevelt told Marshall, after the meeting in Teheran, "I didn't feel I could sleep at ease if you were out of Washington." Eisenhower got the nod.

The long-awaited D-Day invasion across the English Channel finally occurred on June 6, 1944. It was, Churchill observed, "the most difficult and complex operation that has ever taken place." After extensive planning, the Allies waited only for a break in the weather, then landed 156,000 men on five beaches on the Normandy coast of France. In the face of desperate resistance, Eisenhower's forces established a beachhead and used it to bring over more men and equipment; by the end of July there were one-and-a-half million troops, poised to liberate France and keep moving east toward Germany. The day after the D-Day invasion, Stalin told Roosevelt that the Soviet summer campaign would begin by the middle of the month.

This was "a little later than we hoped for," Roosevelt told Churchill, "but it may be for the best in the long run." Germany would face the Russians from the east and the British and Americans from the west in the final campaign.

Roosevelt and Churchill, however, had a major disagreement over strategy as they looked toward Germany. Churchill wanted to keep some troops in Italy to finish mopping up there, after what had turned into a long and frustrating confrontation with the enemy, and also to serve as a bulwark against the Soviets, who were securing their position in Eastern Europe. Roosevelt, less fearful of the Soviet Union, was adamant that the focus needed to be on Germany itself, and wanted the troops eyed by Churchill to invade southern France. He wrote to the prime minister: "At Teheran we agreed upon a definite plan of attack. That plan has gone well so far. Nothing has occurred to require any change. Now that we are fully involved in our major blow history will never forgive us if we lost precious time and lives in indecision and debate. My dear friend, I beg you to let us go ahead with our plan."

The attack continued as Churchill backed down. The Allies liberated Paris by the end of August and looked ahead to Germany, confident the end was in sight. Then German resistance stiffened, as Hitler launched a counteroffensive in December in the Ardennes Forest in eastern France. Although they were fighting back, the Germans still suffered huge casualties in the Battle of the Bulge as the Allied campaign ground on. At the same time, a massive Allied bombing campaign in early February 1945 killed 25,000 civilians in Berlin. Another assault on Dresden 10 days later caused a firestorm that killed 35,000 more. At the end of April, Hitler recognized the certainty of defeat and took his own life. On May 8, Germany surrendered, bringing the Third Reich to an ignominious end.

The end of the war in Europe made the horrendous fate of the Jews starkly visible. Hitler had recorded his anti-Semitism in *Mein Kampf*, and then in the 1930s he had embarked on what became a relentless campaign of extermination of the Jews. Reports in the American press early in the decade documented the growing persecution that led thousands to flee from their homes in Europe before it was too late. But often there was nowhere to go. "The German authorities are treating the Jews shamefully," Roosevelt told William E. Dodd, his new ambassador to Germany, in 1933. "Whatever we can do to moderate the general persecution by unofficial and personal influence ought to be done. But this is also not a governmental affair. We can do nothing except for American citizens."

Nor was the United States willing to do much to help refugees come to America. The restrictive 1924 National Origins Act effectively closed the door on open immigration and imposed strict limits on the number of new entrants to the country. Anti-Semitism made some Americans unwilling to extend assistance to Jews anywhere in the world, while others were simply not interested in the fate of the Jews. Within the State Department, the obstructionist tactics of Assistant Secretary of State Breckinridge Long prevented the easing of restrictive quotas for much of the war. In 1938, FDR ordered special expediting of visa applications that allowed about 50,000 Jews to escape Europe, and he called for an international conference to deal with ways of absorbing Jewish refugees, though he limited the possibility of taking bold action by declaring that "no country would be expected to receive greater numbers of emigrants than is permitted by its existing legislation." The conference occurred, but failed to have a lasting effect. The next year, the *St. Louis*, a Hamburg-American line vessel carrying 930 Jewish refugees, steamed first to Cuba, then up and down the

Atlantic coast of the United States, without being able to land. Finally it took the refugees back to Europe where they faced a grim future.

In early 1944, Treasury officials finally documented the systematic refusal of the State Department to help in any way in a "Report to the Secretary on the Acquiescence by This Government in the Murder of the Jews." Henry Morgenthau brought the report to Roosevelt's attention, and the president responded by creating the War Refugee Board. It helped save some victims, but by the time it was created millions had already died, and the number swelled to 6 million before the war was over. Roosevelt took minimal steps, but thanks to a combination of disbelief at the magnitude of the Nazi effort, unwillingness to confront his own administrative officials, and single-minded concentration on what he felt were the larger issues of the war, he remained insensitive to the plight of people he might have helped. Although he never had a great deal of latitude to act on behalf of the Jews, his reluctance to act more aggressively on their behalf is one of the major blemishes on both his conduct as commander-in-chief and his presidency itself.

As the end of the European war approached, Roosevelt, Churchill, and Stalin met once more, this time in February 1945, at Yalta in the Crimea. Tensions among the three Allies were surfacing even more than before as they looked ahead to the postwar era. Together they decided on dividing Germany into four zones, as well as dividing Berlin, which was located inside the Soviet sector, into four zones, with the United States, the Soviet Union, Great Britain, and France as the occupying powers. They agreed on further discussions about reparations after the war. They talked about the shape of a new world organization to be created and the way the major powers might exercise a veto over issues they found troubling.

Roosevelt met with Churchill (on the left) and Stalin (on the right) at Yalta in early 1945. FDR was not in good health and looked gaunt in this photograph.

The Allies also grappled at Yalta with the question of what to do about Poland, where the German invasion had started the war. As they considered the Russian-Polish border, they agreed that the Soviet Union could take some additional territory and compensate Poland with German land, though, as Churchill remarked, "It would be a pity to stuff the Polish goose so full of German food that it died of indigestion." The more difficult question concerned the shape of the new Polish government. There were two Polish governments in exile, one in Lublin, recognized by the Soviets, the other in London, recognized by the Americans and the British. In the end, the British and Americans accepted the Soviet demand that the Lublin committee form the basis of a new government, with the addition of "some democratic leaders from Polish émigré circles." Roosevelt was reluctant to push the Russians harder, for he wanted their support in organizing a new international organization—to be called the United Nations—to help keep the peace after the war. When Admiral Leahy looked at the final report on Poland, he said, "Mr. President, this is so elastic that the Russians can stretch it all the way from Yalta to Washington without ever technically breaking it." Roosevelt responded, "I know Bill, I know it. But it's the best I can do for Poland at this time."

All the while the United States was fighting alongside its Allies in Europe, it was struggling by itself with the Japanese in the Pacific. That was primarily a naval conflict. The Japanese had used naval power to create their empire, and had deployed naval power in their surprise attack on Pearl Harbor. The United States, with its Pacific fleet in shambles, had to rebuild its own naval capability to be able to roll back the Japanese.

At the start of the war, just as in Europe, the enemy won a series of quick victories. At about the same time as the Pearl Harbor strike, Japan launched air attacks on the Philippines, Guam, and Wake Island—American possessions—and on Burma, Malaya, and Hong Kong—British colonies—and occupied the independent kingdom of Thailand as well. Between December 1941 and the spring of 1942, the Japanese consolidated their gains and imposed their control. For the United States, the fall of the Philippines was worst of all. An American possession since the Spanish-American War of 1898, it was moving on the road to self-government at the time of the Japanese invasion. Forced to evacuate, General Douglas MacArthur pledged, "I shall return."

Six months into the war, *Time* magazine underscored the precarious position in the Pacific. The United States had, it said, "Not taken a single inch of enemy territory, not yet beaten the enemy in a major battle of land, not yet opened an offensive campaign." Hard work lay ahead.

Gradually, the United States struck back at Japan. A bombing raid in April 1942, led by Lieutenant Colonel James H. Doolittle and launched from aircraft carriers in the Pacific, reminded the Japanese that they were vulnerable to air attack. Then, in June 1942, the United States won a crucial naval encounter in the Battle of Midway. Hoping to consolidate Japanese power, Admiral Isoroko Yamamoto, architect of the Pearl Harbor attack, had decided to invade Midway, a small coral island under American control, from which the Japanese could threaten the Hawaiian Islands and, at the same time, draw the United States into a fight that could complete the destruction of the American fleet. Having broken the Japanese code, the United States knew about the forthcoming attack and denied Japan the benefit of surprise. In a bitter battle fought largely in the air, the American navy dealt Japan its first defeat in what was a shift in the momentum of the Pacific war.

As it looked around for a place to launch its own offensive, the United States had its hands full. It wanted to drive the Japanese out of Burma, to help the British defend India, and to protect China, although that latter effort was increasingly difficult because Chiang Kai-shek's Chinese regime was inefficient, corrupt, and under constant challenge by the Chinese Communists. Meanwhile, Admiral Ernest J. King, known for the legendary comment that whenever leaders got into trouble, "they always send for the sons of bitches," was eager to counter a prospective Japanese move against Guadalcanal, in the Solomon Islands, which could provide access to Australia. And Douglas MacArthur, a talented general with a monumental sense of self-importance, wanted help for his efforts to regain the initiative in the Pacific theater. Though Roosevelt had agreed on the strategy of winning the war in Europe first, as the United States invaded Guadalcanal in August 1942 and a long campaign got underway, he ordered that "every possible weapon" be sent there. As the Japanese were driven off the island, Roosevelt cabled Stalin, who was always uncomfortable about efforts that withdrew resources away from engagement in Europe: "We have probably broken the backbone of the power of their Fleet. They still have too many aircraft carriers to suit me, but soon we may well sink some more of them." Much to his relief, FDR understood that "the turning point in this war has been reached."

As Japan settled into a defensive posture, the United States took the offensive. It sank more merchant-shipping tonnage than the Japanese could replace. And it settled on a three-pronged approach to Japan itself: it prepared to attack through China and Southeast Asia; it launched an island campaign northward from Australia into the Philippines; and it mounted an island-hopping operation in the western Pacific. Relentlessly, the island campaign took the Gilbert Islands, then the Marshall Islands, and finally the Marianas. Meanwhile, MacArthur moved from New Guinea into the Philippines, returning to the archipelago as he had pledged. Only Iwo Jima and Okinawa stood in the way of an attack on the Japanese home islands themselves. In the face of fanatical resistance, including suicidal *kamikaze* air attacks on American ships, the United States took both Iwo Jima and Okinawa in the first six months of 1945.

Now just the home islands remained. In early 1945, General Curtis LeMay, head of the Bomber Command, reluctantly abandoned his commitment to ineffective precision bombing of industrial targets in favor of incendiary bombing of Japanese cities. In March, more than 300 B-29s dropped bombs over Tokyo, igniting a ferocious firestorm that destroyed much of the city and killed nearly 90,000 people. Similar campaigns leveled other cities. The European war was grinding to an end and the Pacific war was approaching its conclusion.

9

The War at Home

Franklin Roosevelt had understood the monumental demands of modern warfare when he committed the United States to become the "arsenal of democracy" in 1940. Enormous industrial production was necessary to provide the weapons to win the war. And so, even before the attack on Pearl Harbor, the president began the process of restructuring the industrial sector. Spending huge sums of money restored economic health, just as John Maynard Keynes had predicted it would, and, as the economy operated at full tilt, Americans finally found themselves free from the ravages of the Great Depression. But as the demands of the home front provided new opportunities for groups long denied the benefits of the American dream, it also created dislocations that sometimes threatened to impede the war effort. FDR's job was to provide the leadership to keep all groups working together to achieve the victory over the Axis powers that was their common end. In the process, he also presided over the creation of the modern American state.

Production for war was the nation's first priority. In May 1940, as Roosevelt recognized the need to assist Great Britain in the war against the Axis powers, he asked Congress for $1 billion to produce 50,000 planes; he soon returned to Capitol Hill with a request for even more money. He wanted "speed and speed now," but large-scale production took months, even years, to orchestrate, for it was a complex process to ensure that scarce resources ended up where they were needed most.

In characteristic fashion, Roosevelt established first one agency, then another, until he finally found a combination that worked. Sometimes the agencies operated at cross-purposes; more often a new one took precedence over an old one. The president's first attempt to direct the economy came in 1939, when he created a War Resources Board to assess American needs. Yet, still concerned about isolationist sentiment and wary of full-scale planning, he withheld his own support for a major production effort. "I do not believe that there is an awful lot of Government action that is needed at the present time," he declared in May 1940.

The German blitzkrieg that swept through the Low Countries and France soon after forced FDR to change his mind. Recognizing the importance of better coordination, he resurrected the National Defense Advisory Commission that had helped with mobilization during World War I. But it failed to provide the necessary supervision, for it was only an advisory body without an effective head.

Roosevelt next created the Office of Production Management, in early 1941, to try to stimulate industrial production and resolve problems of the allocation of manpower and raw materials. To lead the new organization, he appointed codirectors—William Knudsen of General Motors and Sidney Hillman of the Amalgamated Clothing Workers of America—but divided leadership proved complicated and eventually broke down. Even more of a problem was the lack of statutory authority to compel manufacturers to place military needs over civilian desires.

In January 1942, after the attack on Pearl Harbor, Roosevelt told Congress just what was required. "It will not be sufficient for us and the other United Nations to produce a slightly superior supply of munitions to that of Germany, Japan, Italy," he said. "The superiority of the United Nations in munitions and ships must be overwhelming . . . a crushing superiority of equipment in any theater of the world war." Then he set what appeared to be extraordinarily high production goals, asking for 60,000 aircraft in 1942, another 125,000 in 1943, and 120,000 tanks and 55,000 antiaircraft guns in that same period.

At the same time, he reorganized the administrative structure in charge of production, this time creating the War Production Board (WPB). He chose Donald Nelson, a top executive with Sears, Roebuck & Company, to head the new agency, with a mandate to "exercise general responsibility" over the economy. As the government now required industry to convert to military production, the WPB sought to curtail the manufacture of nonessential civilian goods through a system of priorities and preferences. When it permitted the military forces to retain responsibility for procurement, it lost the ability to impose central direction at the very time when such coordination was needed most. Roosevelt's decision to appoint "czars" to deal with shortages in key industries, such as petroleum and rubber, likewise complicated Nelson's task and made his position untenable.

Roosevelt finally found a solution that worked when, in May 1943, he created still another agency, the Office of War Mobilization (OWM), to be led by James F. Byrnes. Byrnes had been a Supreme Court justice, after serving as a senator from South Carolina, but most recently had headed the Office of Economic Stabilization, where he mediated disputes among wartime agencies. Byrnes was neither a businessman nor a technocrat; he was a politician savvy to Washington's ways who knew how to get things done. A WPB official summed up Byrnes's talents:

"Suppose that you and I have a disagreement in arithmetic; you claim that two and two make four, while I claim that two and two makes six. We take it to Jimmy Byrnes for a decision. He's apt to get us both to agree that two and two make five." Roosevelt relied on Byrnes. "Your decision is my decision," the president told him. "There is no appeal. For all practical purposes you will be assistant president." With Brynes in charge of the OWM, FDR finally achieved the industrial coordination he needed.

The nation provided what the president demanded. A year after Pearl Harbor, it was manufacturing more military materiel than all of its enemies combined. A year later, at the Teheran conference of the Big Three, Stalin toasted the industrial accomplishments of the United States: "To American production, without which this war would have been lost." By the middle of 1945, the overall numbers told an impressive story: 80,000 landing craft, 100,000 tanks and armored cars, 300,000 airplanes, 15 million guns, and 41 billion rounds of ammunition.

The United States also produced two atomic bombs. In August 1939, just before the war began in Europe, the eminent physicist Albert Einstein wrote Roosevelt a letter in which he noted the theoretical possibility of creating a nuclear chain reaction and said that "it is conceivable . . . that extremely powerful bombs of a new type may thus be constructed." He also indicated that the Germans were interested in the possibility. "This requires action," FDR told Edwin (Pa) Watson, his military aide, and he established a Uranium Committee, chaired by the director of the National Bureau of Standards. Other committees followed, until the War Department took over developing a bomb in the fall of 1942. The top-secret Manhattan Project, as the endeavor came to be called, was an enormous undertaking, eventually costing $2 billion—at the time a huge sum of money—employing 120,000 people in

37 installations in the United States and Canada. As the program produced the first self-sustaining atomic chain reaction in history, scientists began to realize that construction of a workable bomb was indeed possible. As they followed the progress of the Manhattan Project, both Roosevelt and Secretary of War Stimson understood that the prospective new weapon had tangible diplomatic benefits, and they began to include it in strategic calculations in the final year of the war.

Roosevelt paid particular attention to the various constituent groups involved in the effort to stimulate industrial production. Stimson, a Republican, understood what was necessary to meet the president's industrial requirements. "If you are going to try to go to war, or to prepare for war, in a capitalist country," he observed, "you have got to let business make money out of the process or business won't work." Leaders in charge of industrial mobilization therefore provided business with an important incentive—the cost-plus-a-fixed-fee system, whereby the government guaranteed all development and production costs, and then paid a percentage profit on everything produced. As the government suspended competitive bidding and simply asked chosen firms to make what was necessary without regard to cost, business leaders, who now had no worries about risk, were willing to comply.

Roosevelt also recognized the need to channel workers to jobs where they would be most valuable. To that end, in the spring of 1942, he created the War Manpower Commission (WMC), headed by Paul V. McNutt, former governor of Indiana. Attempts to make personnel assignments compulsory faced political opposition, and a more flexible approach implemented by the fall of 1943 worked better in making sure that workers were available where needed.

The huge productive effort succeeded because the government was willing to spend whatever was necessary to make the implements of war. The money came from both taxation and borrowing. Taxes, which had covered about 30 percent of the costs of World War I, increased and accounted for almost 50 percent of the costs of World War II. Roosevelt's own preference was to use taxes to cover the entire cost, noting at the end of 1942, "I would rather pay one hundred percent of taxes now than push the burden of this war onto the shoulders of my grandchildren," but the tax structure was inadequate, and so the government had to borrow the balance of what was needed. The sale of war bonds was one important source of income. The Treasury Department raised $12.9 billion in a first loan drive in late 1942, $135 billion in the entire series of drives.

In addition to supervising industrial mobilization, Roosevelt had responsibility for maintaining the morale of the American people. He was confident the Allies could win the war as long as Americans across the nation believed in their cause and felt a personal stake in the massive common endeavor. His job was to pull all of the country's men and women together behind a shared goal. That meant guiding the propaganda effort that was a necessary part of the campaign to sustain national morale.

Government propaganda was not a new idea. During World War I, journalist George Creel had headed the Committee on Public Information (CPI) with a mandate from Woodrow Wilson to generate support for America's role in the conflict. The CPI did its job too well, as it portrayed the Germans as barbaric Huns and whipped up hatred of all things German. In the postwar years, as a result of the CPI experience, Americans were wary of propaganda, and the president, a master publicist himself, shared their wariness.

Roosevelt knew that an organized information effort could help convey to people at home and to friends and enemies abroad American aims and values in the war.

Nonetheless, he was determined to keep such an effort circumscribed to avoid the excesses of World War I. When the war broke out in Europe in 1939, he created one information agency after another, just as he had on the mobilization front. He set up an Office of Government Reports in September of that year to serve as a clearinghouse for requests for material about what the government was trying to do. The Division of Information in the Office of Emergency Management, established in March 1941, became the major source of information about the nation's defense activities. When neither of those agencies proved effective, in October 1941, FDR created an Office of Facts and Figures (which went by the unfortunate acronym OFF), superimposed on both predecessor agencies. On the overseas front, in August, he authorized the creation of a Foreign Information Service, under the leadership of playwright Robert Sherwood, in the Office of the Coordinator of Information. With the propaganda program in a state of shambles in the first months of America's formal involvement in the war, Roosevelt pulled all of the agencies together in June 1942 into a new Office of War Information (OWI), headed by the well-known and widely trusted news commentator Elmer Davis. Though OWI never had a great deal of support from the president, it trumpeted the liberal terms of the Four Freedoms and the Atlantic Charter to audiences all over the world. It echoed the president's faith, in his address asking for a declaration of war, that "we will gain the inevitable triumph—so help us God." In everything it did, OWI's basic message, according to Davis, was "that we are coming, that we are going to win, and that in the long run everybody will be better off because we won."

The president knew that the organized propaganda effort aroused partisan opposition. Though critics recognized a potential role for propaganda abroad, as long as it was integrated into the larger military effort, they were suspicious of OWI's domestic branch, which they feared would generate support at home for a fourth term for FDR. In the course of a congressional debate, Democratic Representative Joe Starnes of Alabama called domestic propaganda "a stench to the nostrils of a democratic people." In mid-1943, the coalition of Republicans and Southern Democrats in Congress cut off virtually all funding for domestic propaganda, though it permitted the overseas program to continue.

Despite the efforts of the various propaganda agencies, Roosevelt insisted on maintaining personal responsibility for ensuring the support of the American people. In late April 1942, he sent Congress a detailed economic program that called for higher taxes, war bonds, wage and price controls, and a rationing system to allocate consumer goods in short supply. Above all, he wanted to use those economic initiatives to ensure "an equality of sacrifice." In his second wartime fireside chat, he explained his program in terms people could understand. Not everyone, he said, could fight the enemy abroad, or work in a munitions factory at home, but there is "one front and one battle where everyone in the United States—every man, woman and child—is in action. . . . That front is right here at home, in our daily tasks."

The president told his radio listeners that "to build the factory, to buy the materials, to pay the labor, to provide the transportation, to equip and feed and house the soldiers and sailors and marines, and do all the thousands of things necessary in a war—all cost a lot of money, more money than has ever been spent by any nation at any time in the long history of the world." And then he launched into an explanation of what happened with so much money being spent: "You do not have to be a professor of math or economics to see that if people with plenty of cash start bidding against each other for scarce goods, the price of these goods goes up." He had already created a rationing agency, called first the Office of Price Administration and Civilian Supply and later just the Office of Price Administration (OPA), to hold the line on inflation and spread access to goods in short supply as widely as possible. Now it was necessary to give it more authority to do its job. To that end, through the "General Maximum Price Regulation," prices would be fixed according to base prices the month before.

In speeches, as he sought to persuade Americans of the need for shared sacrifice, FDR highlighted the efforts of soldiers overseas. On one occasion, he described the heroic efforts of Captain Hewitt Wheless, a B-17 pilot who managed to limp back to his airbase with both engines failing after shooting down seven Japanese planes. "As we sit here at home contemplating our own duties," the president said, "let us think and think hard of the example which is being set for us by our fighting men."

Roosevelt also took other action to try to maintain morale. In September 1942, he and Eleanor embarked on a 10-day train trip to visit factories and military camps. Eleanor agreed to come on part of the journey, to return home for a number of public commitments of her own, and then to rejoin her husband. Her appearance, as much as his, generated support for the struggle. In Detroit, the group visited the Chrysler tank arsenal and went through automobile manufacturer Henry Ford's bomber factory at Willow Run. The entourage stopped at Minnesota's Twin Cities and passed through North Dakota and Montana as it headed for the West Coast. In Seattle, the president watched production at the Boeing airplane plant, which made the vitally important B-17 bomber. In Portland, he visited entrepreneur Henry Kaiser's shipyard. Standing next to Kaiser, he declared that he wished "every man, woman and child" in the United States could see what "a wonderful piece of work" the Portland shipyard workers were doing, and then concluded, "With the help of God we are going to see this thing through together." Back in Washington at the beginning of October, Roosevelt told reporters at a press conference about his trip and, the next week, he described the journey further in a nationally broadcast radio address. His most important observation, he said, was that "the American people are united as never before in their determination to do a job and do it well."

Small actions helped sustain morale. As major league baseball faced the prospect of collapse when 4,000 of the 5,700 major and minor league players went into military service, the president recognized its value for sustaining a sense of good cheer, and he encouraged its continuation during the war. Games were played in twilight to allow working fans to attend without violating the ban on playing at night that existed in some places. Teams fielded virtual unknowns, but fans still showed up to follow the men as well as the women who played in the new All-American Girls Professional Baseball League formed in 1943.

FDR also understood the need for a few initial victories that he could use to bolster homefront support once the United States entered the war and faced a difficult uphill struggle. To that end, he authorized the risky Doolittle raid on Tokyo in April 1942 and acceded to Churchill's demand for an initial attack on North Africa later that year, rather than holding out for a cross-channel invasion. After the war, Chief of Staff George Marshall, who reluctantly went along with the president, despite his preference for engaging the Germans sooner and more directly, acknowledged the importance of Roosevelt's effort to keep up morale: "We failed to see that the leader in a democracy has to keep the people entertained. That may sound like the wrong word but it conveys the thought."

Roosevelt gradually became aware of the impact of the war on people who had not always shared the advantages of American life. Women were clearly second-class citizens at the start of the conflict. Working women had lost their jobs more rapidly than men at the start of the Great Depression, though they were often rehired more quickly, especially if they headed their households. But they still faced discrimination in the labor market. The huge productive effort that began in 1940 gave women a chance to move into better positions, although initially industrial jobs remained closed to them. Unconvinced that white males, after years of unemployment, would leave jobs at home to volunteer for military service, employers were reluctant to change traditional hiring practices. They also questioned whether women had the strength for heavy manual labor. The War Department concurred by indicating that defense firms "should not be encouraged to utilize women on a large scale until all available male labor in the area has first been employed." Eleanor recognized the role women could play even before the president. "I feel quite certain," she said in 1941, "that we will use women in many ways as England has done. I think it would save time if we registered women now and analyzed their capabilities and decided in advance where they could be used." The president agreed, but after War Manpower Commission head McNutt told him there were still enough men available, he decided not to proceed with Eleanor's industrial registration plan.

The entrance of millions of men into military service changed the situation. By the latter part of 1942, the WMC actively recruited women for factory work in areas where labor was scarce. The OWI issued appeals to women, underscoring the excitement of working for good wages in a patriotic cause. Eleanor again spoke out. "I'm pretty old, 57 you know, to tell girls what to do with their lives," she said, "but if I were of a debutante age I would go into a factory—any factory where I could learn a skill and be useful." It was important, she noted, for young women to get "every bit of preparation they could to expand their horizons and contribute to their country."

On his inspection trips, FDR was pleased with the number of working women he saw. In his radio address describing his late-1942 railroad trip, he declared, "I was impressed by the large proportion of women employed, doing skilled manual labor running machines. Within less than a year from now, there will probably be as many women as men working in our war production effort."

His observation was close to the mark. As women went to work in the factories, the demographic profile of the labor pool changed. Traditionally, working women had been single and young. Now married women and older women gravitated into the labor force. And as they did so, they moved away from domestic service and into both the military and the manufacturing sector. Their share of manufacturing positions increased from 22 percent in 1940 to 32.7 percent in 1944. In that same period, their share of government jobs rose from 19.4 percent to 38.4 percent.

African Americans likewise wanted to use the war effort to gain greater access to jobs. But they found they had to use pressure tactics to bring the president around. In 1940, their unemployment rate was almost twice that for whites. They had difficulty obtaining skilled positions and held many more unskilled jobs than whites. They encountered humiliations in other ways as well. American soldier Lloyd Brown recalled being turned away from a segregated lunchroom in Salina, Kansas, which was willing to serve German prisoners of war. "This was really happening," he said. "It was no jive talk. The people of Salina would serve these enemy soldiers and turn away black American G.I.s." The *Pittsburgh Courier*, a widely circulated black newspaper, proclaimed a "Double V" campaign—V for Victory against the dictators abroad and V for victory in the struggle for equality at home.

Roosevelt faced such pressure for the first time in January 1941, when A. Philip Randolph, head of the Brotherhood of Sleeping Car Porters, a railroad union, proposed a massive March on Washington with the slogan: "WE LOYAL NEGRO AMERICAN CITIZENS DEMAND THE RIGHT TO WORK AND FIGHT FOR OUR COUNTRY." When they met together in mid-June, Randolph presented the president with a series of demands for an end to discrimination and segregation. FDR was worried about the possibility of violence in Washington, a city with southern values and customs, and tried to use his legendary powers of persuasion to get Randolph to call off the march. Randolph refused without "something concrete, something tangible." Roosevelt finally agreed to issue an executive order that met with Randolph's approval. A week later he signed Executive Order 8802, which declared "that there shall be no discrimination in the employment of workers in defense industries or government because of race, creed, color, or national origin," and he created a Fair Employment Practices Committee (FEPC) to implement the policy.

The FEPC held hearings around the country and had some impact, although it was limited. In the industrial Midwest, for example, when it had the cooperation of local authorities, it helped minimize discrimination in some jobs, but the record was still mixed. The agency produced its most impressive results when the demands of military production forced employers to hire from pools of black workers because other sources of labor were in short supply.

In early 1942, Roosevelt hailed the progress he saw. In shipyards, the number of African-American workers had risen in the past year from 6,000 to 14,000, while in the aircraft industry, which had no black employees in 1940, there were now 5,000 at work. "I look for an acceleration of this improvement, as the demand for labor in our war industries increases," Roosevelt told the Fraternal Council of Negro Churches.

But Roosevelt, as during the New Deal, was determined to be careful, and he wanted to avoid doing anything he feared might impede the war effort. He suppressed a first FEPC report on Office of Education defense training at the suggestion of the War Department. Secretary of War Stimson believed that "Leadership is not embedded in the negro race yet and to try to make commissioned officers to lead men into battle—colored men—is only to work disaster to both." Roosevelt himself acknowledged that the "integrity of our nation and our war aims is at stake in our attitude toward minority groups at home," but declared at the end of 1943, "I don't think, quite frankly, that we can bring about the millenium at this time." When he met with members of the Negro Newspaper Publishers Association in the winter of 1944 and listened to a litany of grievances, he called it a good statement but admitted that "we are up against it." Eleanor continued to speak out vigorously against the discrimination she saw, and FDR refused to "put a stop to Mrs. Roosevelt's stirring up trouble," for he recognized her value in doing what he did not feel he could do himself. Gains were coming: in 1942 black workers constituted three percent of all war workers while in 1945 the figure had risen to eight percent. But in 1943, race riots in Detroit and Harlem, in New York City, made it clear to Roosevelt and to others in the administration that there was still a long way to go.

Other minority groups were less fortunate. Latinos and Native Americans made modest gains, yet remained second-class citizens. The Zoot Suit Riot 1943, in which American sailors stationed in Los Angeles rampaged through the streets seizing Chicanos—Latinos from Mexico—who had allegedly attacked them during a night on the town was a reflection of smoldering racial tensions. While Navajos, who spoke a rare language, served the military as code talkers, they encountered continued discrimination when they returned home. German Americans, who had faced bitter denunciations during World War I, had since assimilated into American society, and they had no such troubles in World War II. Italian Americans, more recently arrived than other European immigrants, chafed when FDR designated them enemy aliens, then were relieved when the designation was lifted in the fall of 1942. But Japanese Americans suffered the most serious attack.

Japanese in the United States, most of them concentrated on the West Coast, faced tremendous hostility after the surprise attack on Pearl Harbor. There were only about 127,000 on the American mainland—roughly one-tenth of one percent of the national population—but they were visible and vulnerable. About 47,000 were *Issei*, first-generation immigrants who had been born abroad and were therefore ineligible for citizenship, while approximately 80,000 were *Nisei*, second-generation American citizens, and *Sansei*, their children, who were also citizens. But there was a long history of racial and ethnic animosity, in California in particular, compounded by an eagerness to acquire the property of Japanese Americans. Signs of anti-Japanese sentiment were noticeable everywhere. Rumors, all unfounded, pointed to signs of sabotage on the Pacific coast. A barbershop in California offered "free shaves for Japs," with the note that it was "not responsible for accidents."

Initially, some groups made efforts to avoid scapegoating the West Coast Japanese. The day after Pearl Harbor, the *Los Angeles Times* declared that most of the Japanese on the mainland were "good Americans, born and educated as such" and predicted that there would be "no riots, no mob law." Attorney General Francis Biddle noted that "I was determined to avoid mass internment and the persecution of aliens that had characterized the First World War."

Toward the end of January, FDR met with Supreme Court Justice Owen Roberts, who had prepared a report on the Pearl Harbor disaster. According to Stimson, who also met with the justice, Roberts felt that the Japanese in Hawaii posed a real threat and warned of possible subversive activity. When the report became public, journalists and other observers took its findings as evidence of Japanese disloyalty on the West Coast as well. The *Los Angeles Times* now demanded relocation of all Japanese, both aliens and American citizens. Columnist W. H. Anderson called the Japanese Americans "vipers" who were loyal to Japan and were a "potential and menacing" danger to the United States. Columnist Harry McLemore was even more outspoken: "I am for immediate removal of every Japanese on the West Coast to a point deep in the interior. I don't mean a nice part of the interior either. Herd 'em up, pack 'em off and give 'em the inside room in the badlands. Let 'em be pinched, hurt, hungry and dead up against it . . . Personally, I hate the Japanese, and that goes for all of them."

Meanwhile, a debate over what to do was taking place among Roosevelt's advisers. General John L. DeWitt, head of the Western Defense Command, met with the governor of California, who wanted the Japanese removed, then told the War Department that he favored the evacuation of all Japanese Americans, both aliens and citizens, from the West Coast. FDR presided over a cabinet meeting at the very end of January that considered the idea of evacuation but came to no decision. Attorney General Biddle remained concerned about civil liberties and wanted to avoid any action against American citizens. Stimson, too, was hesitant and hoped to avoid mass evacuation.

Then pressure for government action intensified. At the start of February, the Office of Facts and Figures released a survey showing a significant percentage of West Coast respondents in favor of strong action to deal with the Japanese. Along with Biddle, Eleanor Roosevelt and Archibald MacLeish, the poet and speechwriter who headed the information agency, tried to organize opposition to mass evacuation; Biddle reported to FDR in person about "the danger of hysteria," but to no avail. Roosevelt turned to Stimson instead, who had finally decided on the need for evacuation of all West Coast Japanese, in the interest of national security. In his diary, FDR wrote: "The second generation Japanese can only be evacuated either as part of a total evacuation, giving access to the areas only by permits, or by frankly trying to put them out on the ground that their racial characteristics are such that we cannot understand or trust even the citizen Japanese. The latter is the fact but I am afraid it will make a tremendous hole in our constitutional system to apply it." Stimson spoke to the president by phone and reported that Roosevelt was "very vigorous" and had told him to go ahead with whatever course of action he thought best. According to John J. McCloy, assistant secretary of war, FDR noted that "there will probably be some repercussions, but it has got to be dictated by military necessity, but as he puts it, 'Be as reasonable as you can.'"

On February 19, Roosevelt signed Executive Order 9066. To provide "every possible protection against espionage and against sabotage to national-defense material, national-defense premises and national-defense utilities," it declared, the secretary of war and his military commanders could "prescribe military areas . . . from which any or all persons may be excluded, and with respect to which, the right of any person to enter, remain in, or leave shall be subject to whatever restrictions" the secretary of war and his commanders chose to impose. But other parts of the country proved unwilling to accept the Japanese.

Roosevelt's next step was the creation of a new agency, the War Relocation Authority (WRA). It forcibly moved 110,000 Japanese Americans to ten detention camps in seven western states. Located in desolate areas, the camps housed the internees in tiny apartments in shoddy wooden barracks. Most facilities were communal. In those stark surroundings, traditional family relationships broke down. In 1943, the WRA devised a system to permit Japanese who showed no sign of disloyalty to leave the camps and find work elsewhere. By the end of 1944, about 35,000, mostly *Nisei*, departed. Trouble developed when the War Department tried to register evacuees for military service, and 28 percent of the still-incarcerated male *Nisei*, angry at what they had to endure, refused to renounce allegiance to the emperor of Japan or indicate their willingness to serve in the armed forces. In response, the government segregated these 18,500 further in another, even harsher camp in Tule Lake, California.

The entire internment was a travesty. Even though the Supreme Court upheld the government's actions in several court cases in 1944, it was, in the words of the American Civil Liberties Union, "the worst single wholesale violation of civil rights of American citizens in our history."

Why had Roosevelt approved the relocation? He was under enormous pressure in the weeks and months after Pearl Harbor, and felt he had to do something in response. He justified this action, as others, on the basis of military necessity, even though that was but a flimsy excuse. Though he had known a number of Japanese in college and in his early years of government service, he shared the attitudes of the larger culture about various ethnic groups, Japanese included, and it was not difficult to accept advice from top members of his staff to take decisive action and move ahead. He made a practical decision, in the midst of a difficult time, but one that showed the same lack of sensitivity as his reluctance to ease restrictive immigration quotas for refugee Jews trying to escape the Holocaust. There was no malice involved, only indifference.

All the while, Roosevelt had to remain aware of political considerations, both to secure necessary legislation and to remain in office. Resistance mounted in the early years of the war as the coalition of Republicans and Southern Democrats gained strength. Though "Congress cannot assume to run the war," Ohio's Republican Robert Taft observed, "it does have the job of reasonable criticism," and that criticism mounted. In the midterm elections of 1942, as prosperity returned, it was easy for people who were working again to forget the assistance the Democrats had given them in the past. Republicans made sizable gains in the House of Representatives, where they won 44 new seats and now held 209 seats to the Democrats' 222, and in the Senate, where they gained 9 additional seats.

A fourth term for Roosevelt would be unprecedented. In 1944, with another election looming while the war was in full swing, FDR was again reluctant to step down. With Harry Truman the compromise choice as his running mate, he prepared himself for one last campaign. Facing Republican nominee Thomas E. Dewey, governor of New York, he articulated his hopes for peace and prosperity in the postwar years. He spoke out in favor of a new international organization—which became the United Nations—to promote future stability and stop the kind of aggression that had led to the war. He also endorsed an economic bill of rights that he had proposed to Congress at the beginning of the year. He wanted a commitment from the government to provide people with useful jobs and adequate wages, as well as decent housing, access to education, and protection from the difficulties of old age, illness, accident, or unemployment. Recognizing the difficulty in securing passage of such a program, Roosevelt proposed extending generous benefits to the one group he knew Congress could not deny—the veterans of the war—and therefore pushed for what became the Servicemen's Readjustment Act—the G.I. Bill—later that year. It provided liberal unemployment benefits, educational assistance, and guaranteed loans for purchase of a small business, farm, or home. It served as the model for the commitment to security and prosperity that Roosevelt wanted for all Americans.

Although his health was not good, FDR threw himself into the campaign. At a banquet given by labor officials in September, he showed that he could still pack a political punch. In a speech broadcast nationwide, he deflected the health issue by acknowledging that since the last campaign, "I am actually four years older, which is a fact that seems to an-*noy some* people." And then, with a deadpan delivery, he addressed Republican charges that he had sent a destroyer to retrieve his dog Fala, accidentally left on one of the Aleutian Islands: "These Republican leaders have not been content with attacks—on me, or my wife, or on my sons. No, not content with that, they now include my little dog, Fala. Well, of course, I don't resent attacks, and my family doesn't resent attacks, but Fala *does* resent them. I am accustomed to hearing malicious falsehoods about myself—such as that old, worm-eaten chestnut that I have represented myself as indispensable. But I think I have a right to resent, to object to libelous statements about my dog."

In the election, Roosevelt won again. His plurality of 3.6 million votes and his 53.4 percent share of the popular vote were down from 1940, but he still won an overwhelming 432–99 electoral vote. The Democrats, who won an additional 22 seats in the House of Representatives and lost one seat in the Senate, had safe majorities, though the Republican-Southern Democratic coalition that had coalesced during the Court-packing fight remained intact.

But Roosevelt's health was precarious. The previous March, as he went for an intensive physical examination with cardiologist Howard G. Bruenn at the Naval Hospital in Bethesda, Maryland, FDR acknowledged, "I feel like hell!" He had trouble breathing in bed, and his hands shook when he held a coffee cup or tried to light a cigarette. An attack of influenza at the end of 1943 left him weak, but the real problem was far more serious. The results of the physical examination showed FDR suffering from hypertension, hypertensive heart disease, and cardiac failure in his left ventricular chamber. His overall health, in Bruenn's assessment, was "God-awful."

As he delivered his fourth and final inaugural address in January 1945, Roosevelt looked pale and gaunt. He had lost about 25 pounds since the summer. He was ill at Yalta, where he negotiated with Churchill and Stalin for the last time, and still felt weak when he returned home. He had helped plan strategy for the greatest war ever fought. He had mobilized a fragmented home front and provided the leadership that kept the American people attuned to the struggle's demands. Now, as the war wound down, he was exhausted.

Epilogue

In April 1945, Roosevelt went to Warm Springs to relax. He knew his health was deteriorating, and he was also lonely. He loved having people around him, particularly in the evening, when he enjoyed mixing drinks and talking casually with friends. Eleanor, busy with her many independent activities, was seldom around, and his secretary, Marguerite (Missy) Le Hand, who had begun to work for FDR in 1920, frequently served as hostess in Eleanor's absence. Like a member of the family, she provided the companionship Roosevelt craved, but she suffered a debilitating stroke in 1941, from which she never fully recovered. Ill herself for most of the war, she could not give FDR the support he needed, and she died in 1944. Nor were other loved ones available. The president's mother, with whom he enjoyed a close relationship all his life, had died in the fall of 1941, and Harry Hopkins, perhaps his closest confidant, had remarried and was spending more time with his new wife.

As he traveled with Eleanor on the inspection trip of the nation's factories in 1942, FDR approached his wife gingerly with a special request. He asked her to stay at home with him, to spend more time together, to serve as hostess at the cocktail hour; in short, to try to live together once more as husband and wife. Eleanor, hurt terribly by her husband's affair with Lucy Mercer years before, thought about the request but ultimately could not comply. In a conversation when they both returned to Washington, she asked for an assignment that would let her move around the country more and visit troops overseas. It was clear to FDR, though she never said so directly, that Eleanor could not come back.

In her place, Roosevelt sometimes relied on his daughter Anna, who served as hostess when she was around. Well aware of her father's need for companionship, without Eleanor's knowledge, Anna helped him renew his relationship with Lucy Mercer Rutherfurd, who had married after her affair with FDR ended and whose husband had recently died. She was present at Warm Springs that April as part of the presidential entourage. On April 12, as FDR sat in the living room posing for a portrait, signing documents, and reading papers, he suddenly held his left temple. "I have a terrific headache," he said, and he slumped over. Still breathing as his doctor and friends carried him into bed, he never revived from the massive cerebral hemorrhage and, several hours later, despite all efforts to save him, he died.

Roosevelt's death was not unexpected to those closest to him. He had been ill when he went to Yalta to confer with Churchill and Stalin, and unable to stand when he told Congress what the conference had accomplished. In the end, he succumbed to the heart disease and high blood pressure that had been diagnosed a year before, but had been kept secret from the public.

A new president—Harry S Truman—had to make the final decisions that brought an end to the war. In an effort to avoid a potentially brutal invasion, Truman rejected other alternatives, such as a blockade, that might have encouraged the Japanese to surrender. Instead, he authorized the use of the new atomic bombs over Japan, killing instantly about 60,000 people in Hiroshima and 35,000 in Nagasaki, and almost as many more from radiation sickness and the lingering aftereffects of the devastating new weapon in the days, weeks, and months that followed. On August 14, the Japanese accepted American terms for surrender, which occurred formally on September 2, on the battleship *Missouri.* The war was finally over, but the world would never again be the same.

Though he was unable to savor the final victory, Roosevelt left a profound mark on the American people and on people around the world. He was the most influential leader in the United States in the twentieth century, and, even after the demise of the Democratic coalition that dominated politics for nearly 40 years, his legacy lived on. At a time when the nation was suffering from the worst economic crisis it had ever known, he restored a sense of hope that everything would be all right in the end. With his willingness to try first one approach, then another, he proved to be one of the most innovative leaders in the nation's history, yet he never lost his fundamentally conservative commitment to the capitalist system he helped to survive. He changed the view Americans had of their government, first with the alphabet agencies of the New Deal, then with the mobilization efforts of World War II, as he presided over the creation of the American welfare state, and underscored the idea that the government would step in to help those who could not help themselves. And he stood up to the dictators in Europe and Asia who threatened the very fabric of democracy and, in the process, presided over the creation of a new world order.

His record was not without flaws. The New Deal never did bring about the recovery it promised, largely because of the exuberant efforts to work in all directions at once. Roosevelt could not comprehend Keynesian economics, and so was never able to make a commitment to the kind of spending program that might have brought revival sooner. He was prepared to compromise on a commitment to racial equality when he felt it was politically necessary, and he was unwilling to explore ways of saving European Jews from the Holocaust or devise a fair way of dealing with the Japanese Americans in the United States.

Early in his career, some observers considered him a political lightweight, in large part because of his almost relentless glibness and good cheer. He belied those early predictions about his future possibilities as he used his optimism successfully in his public appeal for support in hard times and, through his extraordinarily effective use of radio, changed the nature of the relationship between the president and the people of the United States. But even as he clung to the public buoyancy that helped him deal with the damage to his own body and the devastation to the American free-enterprise system and the challenge of the deadly dictators abroad, some people found it difficult to see beyond what they perceived as a mask. After a bitter political fight in a cabinet meeting once, Harold Ickes noted of the president that "despite his very pleasant and friendly personality, he is as cold as ice inside." Perhaps that coldness permitted him to be all things to all people, to make the compromises he deemed politically necessary, to hurt those he loved the most.

But Roosevelt's limitations only highlight the remarkable record of accomplishment he left behind. When he died in 1945, the nation was a very different—and better—place than it had been before.

Study and Discussion Questions

Prologue

1. What were some of the complexities in Franklin Roosevelt's life?

2. Why did some people consider him a paradoxical figure?

Chapter 1: The Roosevelts of Hyde Park

1. What was the background of the Roosevelt family?

2. How did class structure affect the way Franklin Roosevelt was raised?

3. What role did Franklin's mother Sara play in his life?

4. What impressions did FDR convey while he was a student at Groton and later at Harvard?

5. Why do you think Eleanor and Franklin were attracted to one another?

Chapter 2: Political and Personal Affairs

1. Why was Franklin intrigued by the example of his distant cousin Theodore?

2. How successful was Franklin in his first political role in the New York State Senate?

3. How successful was he in his role as assistant secretary of the navy?

4. What effect did Franklin's affair with Lucy Mercer have on his personal and political life?

5. What was the lasting impact of polio on FDR's life?

Chapter 3: Governor of New York

1. Why was Roosevelt originally reluctant to run for governor of New York?

2. In what ways did FDR show his commitment to the progressive tradition in America?

3. How did Roosevelt react to the Great Depression in New York State?

4. How did Roosevelt's actions in New York affect his chances for national political office?

5. What was the effect of Roosevelt's flight to Chicago to address the Democratic national convention in person?

6. Why did Roosevelt win such an overwhelming victory in the presidential election of 1932?

Chapter 4: The First Hundred Days

1. What was the nature of Roosevelt's relationship with Herbert Hoover in the months after the election before he formally took office?

2. What plans did FDR have at the outset for dealing with the problems of the Great Depression?

3. What was the cause of the banking crisis, and what did Roosevelt propose to do about it?

4. What issues did Roosevelt raise in his first inaugural address? What impact did it have?

5. How do you explain the outpouring of support for FDR?

6. What do you consider the most important actions of the first hundred days?

7. How effective an administrator was FDR?

Chapter 5: New Deal Initiatives

1. How well did the NRA work in promoting recovery?

2. How successfully did Roosevelt deal with agricultural questions during the New Deal?

3. How did Roosevelt deal with relief issues in the early years of the New Deal?

4. What were the most important accomplishments of the WPA?

5. Why were conservatives furious with FDR and the New Deal?

6. Who were the most vocal critics of the New Deal, and what was the nature of their critique?

7. Why was Roosevelt so concerned with social security, and what was the nature of his approach?

Chapter 6: Success and Stalemate

1. How did ordinary Americans view FDR?

2. Why did Roosevelt strike out at business interests in the campaign of 1936?

3. How did Roosevelt deal with the recession of 1937?

4. Why was Roosevelt irritated at the Supreme Court? How well did his plan to pack the Court fare? What was its long-term effect?

5. Using the analysis of English economist John Maynard Keynes, how successful were Roosevelt's efforts to achieve recovery?

6. What was Roosevelt's role in shaping the modern American presidency?

Chapter 7: The Road to War

1. What threats to world peace did FDR perceive as he took office in 1933?

2. How did Roosevelt react to the pressure for neutrality legislation?

3. When World War II broke out, why did Roosevelt refuse to ask America to remain neutral in thought as well as deed?

4. What was the nature of Roosevelt's relationship with British Prime Minister Winston Churchill and what impact did it have on American policy?

5. Why did Roosevelt decide to run for a third term?

6. What was Roosevelt's reaction to the Japanese attack on Pearl Harbor?

Chapter 8: Commander-in-Chief

1. How did American entrance into the war change Roosevelt's priorities?

2. What was the nature of the relationship among the three leaders of the Grand Alliance?

3. Why did Roosevelt, Churchill, and Soviet leader Josef Stalin disagree over wartime strategy?

4. Why did Roosevelt acquiesce in attacks on North Africa and then Italy before launching a cross-channel invasion?

5. How did FDR deal with the issue of helping Jews escape from Nazi-dominated Europe? What more could he have done?

Chapter 9: The War at Home

1. What did FDR mean when he spoke about the need for the United States to become the "arsenal of democracy"?

2. How successfully did Roosevelt deal with the issue of mobilization?

3. How did Roosevelt deal with maintaining the morale of the American people? How did he use propaganda to achieve his ends?

4. Why did FDR agree to promote the hiring of more women in the nation's factories?

5. How well did Roosevelt deal with the demands of African Americans for equality during the war?

6. What was Roosevelt's role in the internment of the Japanese Americans? Why did he approve the policy that was finally adopted?

Epilogue

1. What were the weaknesses in Roosevelt's overall record?

2. What was his ultimate legacy?

A Note on the Sources

Any biography of Franklin D. Roosevelt relies on the presidential papers, located at the Franklin D. Roosevelt Presidential Library and Museum in Hyde Park, New York. A helpful staff and comfortable surroundings make it a delightful place to work. The published papers—compiled in 13 volumes by Samuel I. Rosenman under the title *The Public Papers and Addresses of Franklin D. Roosevelt* and found in any major library—are essential, and these documents are now available at The American Presidency Project on the World Wide Web at http://www.presidency.ucsb.edu/. But there is at the same time a rich and voluminous collection of writing about FDR's life and career. What follows are the sources—both old and new—that I found most useful in writing this short volume, along with suggestions for further reading about a variety of the most important personal and political issues FDR faced.

Biographies of Roosevelt abound. For his early life, see Geoffrey C. Ward, *Before the Trumpet: Young Franklin Roosevelt, 1882–1905* (New York: Harper & Row, Publishers, 1985) and *A First-Class Temperament: The Emergence of Franklin D. Roosevelt* (New York: Harper & Row, Publishers, 1989). Another detailed (but never completed) biography titled *Franklin D. Roosevelt* by Frank Freidel includes four volumes: *The Apprenticeship* (Boston:

Little, Brown and Company, 1952); *The Ordeal* (Boston: Little, Brown and Company, 1954); *The Triumph* (Boston: Little, Brown and Company, 1956); and *Launching the New Deal* (Boston: Little, Brown and Company, 1973). A readable five-volume account by Kenneth S. Davis covers most of Roosevelt's life: *FDR: The Beckoning of Destiny, 1882–1928: A History* (New York: G. P. Putnam's Sons, 1972); *FDR: The New York Years, 1928–1933* (New York: Random House, 1985); *FDR: The New Deal Years, 1933–1937: A History* (New York: Random House, 1986); *FDR: Into the Storm, 1937–1940: A History* (New York: Random House, 1993); and *FDR: The War President, 1940–1943: A History* (New York: Random House, 2000). James MacGregor Burns was one of the earliest Roosevelt biographers and both *Roosevelt: The Lion and the Fox* (New York: Harcourt, Brace & World, Inc., 1956) and *Roosevelt: The Soldier of Freedom, 1940–1945* (New York: Harcourt Brace Jovanovich, Inc., 1970) remain useful. Conrad Black's *Franklin Delano Roosevelt: Champion of Freedom* (New York: Public Affairs, 2003) is a recent retelling of Roosevelt's story, more helpful than Roy Jenkins' very brief account (completed after his death by Arthur M. Schlesinger, Jr.), *Franklin Delano Roosevelt* (New York: Henry Holt and Company, 2003). A more thorough short account of FDR's life is George McJinsey, *The Presidency of Franklin D. Roosevelt* (Lawrence: University Press of Kansas, 2000).

On Eleanor Roosevelt, the necessary starting point is Joseph P. Lash, *Eleanor and Franklin: The story of their relationship based on Eleanor Roosevelt's private papers* (New York: W. W. Norton & Company, Inc., 1971). Blanche Wiesen Cook, *Eleanor Roosevelt, Volume One, 1884–1933* (New York: Viking, 1992) and *Eleanor Roosevelt, Volume Two, 1933–1938* (New York: Viking, 1999) are both useful. Equally engaging is the brief biography in this Library of American Biography series, J. William T. Youngs, *Eleanor Roosevelt: A Personal and Public Life*

Second Edition (New York: Pearson Longman, 2000). Eleanor's own account, *The Autobiography of Eleanor Roosevelt* (New York, Harper & Brothers Publishers, 1958), provides her perspective on her life. For two recent books about FDR's relationship with Lucy Mercer, and its impact on Eleanor's relationship with Franklin, see Ellen Feldman, *Lucy* (New York: W. W. Norton & Company, 2003) and Resa Willis, *FDR and Lucy: Lovers and Friends* (New York: Routledge, 2004).

The best book dealing with the entire Roosevelt era, which pays close attention to FDR's own contributions, is David M. Kennedy, *Freedom from Fear: The American People in Depression and War, 1929–1945* (New York: Oxford University Press, 1999). Richard D. Polenberg, *The Era of Franklin D. Roosevelt, 1933–1945: A Brief History with Documents* (New York: Bedford/St. Martin's, 2000) contains a first-rate introduction on "Franklin D. Roosevelt and American Liberalism" and a helpful compilation of the most important documents from his presidency.

In examining the New Deal, William E. Leuchtenburg, *Franklin D. Roosevelt and the New Deal* (New York: Harper & Row, Publishers, 1963) remains indispensable, still useful 40 years after its publication. Also still well worth reading is Arthur M. Schlesinger, Jr.'s powerful three-volume trilogy under the general title *The Age of Roosevelt*, which includes: *The Crisis of the Old Order, 1919–1933* (Boston: Houghton Mifflin Company, 1957); *The Coming of the New Deal* (Boston: Houghton Mifflin Company, 1958); and *The Politics of Upheaval* (Boston: Houghton Mifflin Company, 1960). Robert S. McElvaine, *The Great Depression: America, 1929–1941* (New York: Times Books, 1993) is a thoughtful and more recent account, while Anthony J. Badger, *The New Deal: The Depression Years, 1933–1940* (New York: The Noonday Press—Farrar, Straus & Giroux, 1989) is likewise a helpful treatment. On New Deal economic policy, see Ellis

Hawley, *The New Deal and the Problem of Monopoly* (Princeton: Princeton University Press, 1966). John Morton Blum, *From the Morgenthau Diaries* amplifies on economic issues through the eyes of Henry Morgenthau, secretary of the treasury during much of FDR's presidency, in three important volumes: *Years of Crisis, 1928–1938* (Boston: Houghton Mifflin Company, 1959); *Years of Urgency, 1938–1941* (Boston: Houghton Mifflin Company, 1965); and *Years of War, 1941–1945* (Boston: Houghton Mifflin Company, 1967). Perhaps even more accessible is the one-volume version: *Roosevelt and Morgenthau: A Revision and Condensation of From the Morgenthau Diaries* (Boston: Houghton Mifflin Company, 1970). On the impact of Keynes, see Robert S. Lekachman, *The Age of Keynes* (New York: Vintage Books—A Division of Random House, 1968). For a still perceptive examination of New Deal labor policy, see Irving Bernstein, *Turbulent Years: A History of the American Worker, 1933–1941* (Boston: Houghton Mifflin Company, 1969). Harvard Sitkoff, ed., *Fifty Years Later: The New Deal Evaluated* (New York: Alfred A. Knopf, 1985) is a thoughtful collection of essays by various historians looking back at the period.

Roosevelt's use of the radio helped connect him to the American people, particularly during the New Deal, and two books provide a good start to the powerful—and positive—responses he generated. Robert S. McElvaine, *Down & Out in the Great Depression: Letters from the Forgotten Man* (Chapel Hill: The University of North Carolina Press, 1983) is a useful collection of letters to the president from all sectors of society. Lawrence W. Levine and Cornelia R. Levine, *The People and the President: America's Conversation with FDR* (Boston: Beacon Press, 2002) is an equally helpful collection of letters to the White House.

On Roosevelt's fight with the Supreme Court, and its impact on reform, two key books are William E. Leuchtenburg, *The Supreme Court Reborn: The Constitutional*

Revolution in the Age of Roosevelt (New York: Oxford University Press, 1995) and Barry Cushman, *Rethinking the New Deal Court: The Structure of a Constitutional Revolution* (New York: Oxford University Press, 1998).

For Roosevelt's approach to diplomacy, Robert Dallek, *Franklin D. Roosevelt and American Foreign Policy, 1932–1945* (New York: Oxford University Press, 1979) is an excellent starting point. Primary materials can be found in various volumes of *Foreign Relations of the United States*. Another useful documentary collection is Edgar B. Nixon, ed., *Franklin D. Roosevelt and Foreign Affairs*, 3 vols. (Cambridge: Belknap Press of Harvard University Press, 1969). Two brief but helpful accounts of the coming of the war are: Robert A. Divine, *The Reluctant Belligerent: American Entry into World War II*, 2nd ed. (New York: John Wiley & Sons, 1979) and Justus D. Doenecke and John E. Wiltz, *From Isolation to War, 1931–1941*, 2nd ed. (Arlington Heights, Illinois: Harlan Davidson, Inc., 1991). A similarly brief but useful introduction to fighting in the war itself is Gary R. Hess, *The United States at War, 1941–1945* (Arlington Heights, Illinois: Harlan Davidson, Inc., 1986). For Roosevelt's relationship with Winston Churchill, see Jon Meacham, *Franklin and Winston: An Intimate Portrait of an Epic Friendship* (New York: Random House, 2003). On the administration's response to the Holocaust, several books provide a good introduction: Henry I. Feingold, *The Politics of Rescue: The Roosevelt Administration and the Holocaust, 1938–1945* (New Brunswick, New Jersey: Rutgers University Press, 1970) and David Wyman, *Paper Walls: America and the Refugee Crisis, 1938–1941* (Amherst: University of Massachusetts Press, 1968) and *The Abandonment of the Jews: America and the Holocaust, 1941–1945* (New York: Pantheon Books, 1984).

In examining the home front, a number of books are useful. Two older but still timely treatments are Richard

Polenberg, *War and Society: The United States, 1941–1945* (Philadelphia: J. B. Lippincott, 1972) and John Morton Blum, *V Was for Victory: Politics and American Culture during World War II* (New York: Harcourt Brace Jovanovich, 1976). More recent volumes worth attention are Allan M. Winkler, *Home Front U.S.A.: America during World War II*, 2nd ed. (Wheeling, Illinois: Harlan Davidson, Inc., 2000) and John W. Jeffries, *Wartime America: The World War II Home Front* (Chicago, Ivan R. Dee, 1996).

There is a growing literature on specific wartime issues. For Eleanor and Franklin's partnership during the war, see Doris Kearns Goodwin, *No Ordinary Time: Franklin and Eleanor Roosevelt: The Home Front in World War II* (New York: Simon & Schuster, 1994). On women and the war, William Henry Chafe, *The American Woman: Her Changing Political, Economic and Social Role in the Twentieth Century* (New York: Oxford University Press, 1972) remains a good starting point. Also worth examining are: Susan M. Hartmann, *The Homefront and Beyond: American Women in the 1940s* (Boston: Twayne Publishers, 1982); Karen Anderson, *Wartime Women, Sex Roles, Family Relations, and the Status of Women during World War II* (Westport, Connecticut: Greenwood Press, 1982); and D'Ann Campbell, *Women at War with America: Private Lives in a Patriotic Era* (Cambridge: Harvard University Press, 1984). On African Americans, a good place to begin remains Neil Wynn, *The Afro-American and the Second World War* (New York: Holmes & Meier Publishers, 1976). On the Japanese American internment, see the brief but perceptive treatment by Roger Daniels, *Prisoners without Trial: Japanese Americans in World War II*, revised edition (New York: Hill and Wang, 2004) and a useful account by Greg Robinson, *By Order of the President: FDR and the Internment of Japanese Americans* (Cambridge: Harvard University Press, 2001).

Index